A STUDY GUIDE TO

GREATER BIBLE KNOWLEDGE

By **WAYNE JACKSON**

Courier Publications
7809 N. Pershing Ave.
Stockton, CA 95207

ISBN 0-9678044-9-3

DEDICATION

To:

Diane Moore and Janie Craun

The Lord has blessed me with two wonderful sisters in the flesh. In their childhood years, I was, doubtless, a vexation to their souls. It is my fond hope that they now realize how very dearly their older brother loves them.

TABLE OF CONTENTS

1. The Importance of Effective Bible Study 1
2. The Theme of the Bible 10
3. Principles of Bible Interpretation 20
4. Periods of Bible History 30
5. The Books of the Bible — An Overview 44
6. Analyzing the Books of the Bible 56
7. Analyzing the Bible by Chapters 69
8. Tools for Bible Study 83
9. Accurate Biblical Exegesis 98
10. The Study of Biblical Words 109
11. Comparative Bible Study 119
12. Topical Bible Studies 130
13. Biographical Bible Studies 145

Chapter 1

THE IMPORTANCE OF EFFECTIVE BIBLE STUDY

The New Testament writer James affirmed: "Every good gift and every perfect gift is from above, coming down from the Father of lights...." (James 1:27). Certainly the benevolence of our great God is evidenced in a multitude of ways, and not the least of these is the gift of his divine word, the Bible.

Jehovah has revealed himself to man in a remarkable number of ways. His existence is apparent in nature (Psalms 19:1; Romans 1:20), by means of his providence (Acts 14:17), in the human conscience (Romans 2:14, 15), and, of course, through his Son, Jesus of Nazareth (John 1:18). Additionally, however, our Creator has spoken to man through a series of inspired documents collectively called the Bible.

The Bible is a book to be studied and revered. This hallowed volume is not held in high esteem simply due to its antiquity. The classical writings of ancient Greece are hoary with age, yet precious few people have the interest, or take the time, to explore their dusty pages. But such is not the case with the Bible. It is the most studied narrative in the world! Intelligent people are interested in its history and its gripping message. There surely must be a reason for such keen excitement concerning the Bible. Indeed, there is. It is a book ultimately from Heaven!

One of the best known laws of the universe is the law of cause and effect. Simply stated, it is this: every **effect** must

1

have an adequate **cause**. Now let this rule be applied to the
Bible. The Bible is an effect; it is here. It was caused by some
source. Really, there are but two possibilities: (a) The Scriptures originated from a purely **human** source; or, (b) The Bible,
though employing human writers, is nonetheless ultimately
of divine origin. How can one determine which of these views
is correct? The only way is to examine the document itself and
see whether or not it bears those marks of identification which
would be demanded of a book that originated with God. What
would be expected of a **divine** volume? Let us consider this
thought momentarily.

First, if God gave the Bible, we would expect him to tell
us so. The fact is, he has done just that. More than 3,800 times
in the Old Testament alone, there are claims that the Scriptures
are ultimately from Jehovah. For example, "And Jehovah said
unto Moses, Write this for a memorial book...." (Exodus 17:
14). The book of Leviticus abounds with affirmations of its
divine origin. Twenty of the twenty-seven chapters begin with
the words, "And Jehovah spake unto Moses saying...." Jesus
Christ himself endorsed the concept that the Old Testament
is a divinely inspired composition. The Lord, citing from the
book of Exodus, declared: "Have ye not read that which was
spoken unto you by God?" (Cf.: Matthew 22:31). A similar
exalted claim is made by the writers of the New Testament
literature. For instance, Paul, addressing the Christian brotherhood in Thessalonica, commended them in that they had received his message "not as the word of men, but, as it is in
truth, the word of God" (I Thessalonians 2:13). Peter contended that the writings of his beloved brother, Paul, were
"scripture" (II Peter 3:16)—and the word "scripture" in the
Bible is used as a technical term for a **divinely inspired** writing.
God is, therefore, according to his own testimony, the ultimate Author of the Bible.

Second, if God is the source of the Bible, since he is perfect (Matthew 5:48), and is not the author of confusion or con-
tradiction (Cf.: I Corinthians 14:33), we would expect it to be

perfectly harmonious. Such is precisely the case. The Bible is a grand scheme of unity in theme, plan, doctrine, historical details, etc. Since the sixty-six books of the sacred volume were penned over a span of sixteen hundred years, by some forty different individuals, this profound oneness is nothing short of miraculous. For a more detailed discussion of this matter, see my book, *Fortify Your Faith*, pp 58ff. Moreover, while it is true that some hostile critics allege that the biblical writers sometimes contradict themselves and other writers of scripture, such charges simply will not stand the test of honest and scholarly investigation.

Third, since God is holy (Isaiah 6:3), we would expect the Bible to have an exalted moral tone. This is just what one discovers. Its precepts—"love your neighbor as yourself" and "do unto others as you would have them do unto you" (Matthew 22:39; 7:12)—have amazed and challenged multitudes for centuries. No other religious philosophy in all the world has the high moral emphasis that is characteristic of the Word of God.

Fourth, if the Bible is from God, we would not expect that any group of men, regardless of their genius, could produce a volume that would surpass that ancient document. If someone is able, let him "write one up"! The world is waiting. Though the Scriptures have been completed for nineteen centuries, no one has yet been able to author a book for living that would make the Bible obsolete. This is utterly inexplicable!

Fifth, if the Bible came from the timeless God (Psalms 90:2), we would expect it to be perpetually relevant. Books of men, though written by the finest scholars, are generally outdated in only a few years, but the Holy Scriptures are as fresh as when they issued from inspired pens. Who can explain, on a solely natural basis, why a book nineteen centuries old (in its completed form) should be the twentieth century bestseller?

Sixth, if the Bible is of divine origin, we would expect it

to accurately portray the character of man. This is exactly what it does. Though man was created upright (Ecclesiastes 7:29), in God's own image (Genesis 1:26), by sin he has progressively separated himself from his Maker (Isaiah 59:1, 2). He has become exceedingly corrupt (Jeremiah 17:9), and hence stands in dire need of help. Man could not have authored the Bible if he would, and would not have penned it if he could. Human philosophy contends that man has clawed his way upward (compare the theory of evolution), but the Word of God reveals man in his true light—a fallen creature.

Seventh, if the Bible is from God, we would not expect it to simply be a vague philosophical and abstract treatise, but rather, that it would give specific information concerning the purpose of man, and how that purpose may be achieved. It does just this, and this is why it is so essential to diligently and correctly study this Holy Book.

In view of the foregoing considerations (that is, that the Bible is an oracle from Heaven), the obvious need to investigate this sacred production is paramount. But let us note some of the specific values in carefully studying the Scriptures.

(1) Man is a curious creature. He wants to know from whence he came; he is ever searching for his "roots" (no other organism has this interest). Moreover, it is generally recognized that whatever view one has regarding his origin, the same will be reflected in his conduct. For instance, if he believes that he is but a brute beast, and if he logically pursues this inclination, he will live on the animal level. And thousands are doing just that! On the other hand, when humanity learns of its lofty beginning, and the responsibility that mankind sustains to the Creator, many can be directed back to the Almighty. The question of "origins" is thus vitally important, and there is no source, other than the Bible, for securing this information.

(2) No human being can live happily without purpose. A man with no sense of direction is an aimless, pathetic individual. The Bible reveals our purpose. We are not destined to live our frail, threescore and ten only to pass into oblivion. We were

created for eternity and our ultimate contentment is only to be found in serving God. We are made for His glory (Isaiah 43:7). Solomon expressed it in this fashion: "This is the end of the matter; all hath been heard: Fear God, and keep his commandments; for this is the whole duty of man. For God will bring every work into judgment, with every hidden thing, whether it be good, or whether it be evil" (Ecclesiastes 12:13, 14). Man thus came from God; he is under obligation to serve his Creator; and, he will meet the Lord finally in Judgment. The biblical narrative burns this dramatic message into our hearts. Are we wise enough to listen?

(3) The Bible is the record of the greatest Person who ever lived on Earth. It contains the history of Jesus of Nazareth, the divine Son of God. Though the existence and history of Christ can clearly be documented from the writings of the ancient past—Jewish, Greek and Roman—, nothing, outside of the New Testament record, really reveals his character and the purpose of his mission. Without Christ, no person can come into fellowship with the God of the Universe (John 14:6), and without the Bible no one can "know" Christ, as that term is biblically used (I John 2:3).

(4) The Bible is designed to innoculate against personal sin. The Psalmist acknowledged: "Thy word have I laid up in my heart, that I might not sin against thee" (Psalms 119:11). Again, "The law of his God is in his heart; none of his steps shall slide" (Psalms 37:31). If our minds were filled with holy truth, undoubtedly we would be more fortified against the enemy of our souls. When the Savior was thrice assaulted by the Devil, he resisted sin on each occasion with a resounding, "It is written!" (Matthew 4:1-11). The man who meditates day and night upon Jehovah's word is like a fruitful tree planted by streams of water (Psalms 1:3). In his own self-interest, therefore, one needs to learn sound principles of Bible study.

(5) Some have never seen a false teacher. They think no such creature exists. Christ, though, entertained no such no-

tion, for he plainly taught: "Beware of false prophets, who come to you in sheep's clothing, but inwardly are ravening wolves" (Matthew 7:15). There is a difference between truth and error. Truth is truth; error is error; and never the twain shall meet. And those who believe and yield to error will clearly be lost; nothing in the Bible is plainer than that (Cf.: II Thessalonians 2:11, 12). But how does one discern the truth of God from satanic lies (Cf.: John 8:44)? Only in the light of Scripture.

Consider this example. The ancient Sadducees denied that the dead would be raised from the grave. In a discussion with these modernists, Christ pointed out that their problem resulted from the fact that they **knew not the Scriptures** nor the power of God (Matthew 22:29). Multiplied scores of souls are seduced daily by advocates of false religion simply because they are not grounded in the basic teaching of the Word of God. More need to follow the example of the discriminating citizens of Beroea, who, upon hearing a new religious teaching, examined what they heard in the light of the Scriptures to determine whether or not the instruction was accurate (Acts 17:11). The ancient proclamation: "My people are destroyed for a lack of knowledge" (Hosea 4:6) was never more true than today! The Bible needs to be diligently studied to stay the progress of religious error.

(6) The Christian, through his response to the gospel (Acts 2:38; Hebrews 5:9), has become a recipient of the grace of Christ. Thereby, he becomes a debtor to all men (Romans 1:14), that they too might taste the sweet springs of salvation. Bearing fruit is a divine obligation. Jesus told his disciples: "Every branch in me that beareth not fruit, he taketh it away; and every branch that beareth fruit, he cleanseth it, that it may bear more fruit" (John 15:2). Through our conversion, we have become joined to the Lord in order that we might bring forth offspring unto God (Cf.: Romans 7:4). If one is to lead the lost to the Lord Jesus, and then guide them toward spiritual maturity, he must be qualified for this noble task, and

that involves having a good working knowledge of the Scriptures. You cannot teach what you do not know. The Bible is thus designed to equip us for the noble labor of winning souls. Listen to these ringing words of the apostle: "Every scripture is inspired of God, and profitable for teaching, for reproof, for correction, for instruction which is in righteousness: that the man of God my be complete, furnished completely unto every good work" (II Timothy 3:16, 17). What a sobering responsibility to represent oneself as a teacher of God's Word. Far too many want the acclaim which commonly attaches to being a good teacher, and yet, frequently without taking the necessary time to qualify for such an awesome task. Let us be sobered with these words: "Be not many of you teachers, my brethren, knowing that we shall receive heavier judgment" (James 3:1). This was not written to discourage us from teaching, but to stress the gravity thereof.

(7) We live in a world of woe. There is disease and death. There is anguish and anxiety. There is sorrow and sighing. Our rebellion against God has many attendant evils (Cf.: Romans 5:12). Though we all may attempt to work for better conditions on this earth, we must finally concede, with stark reality, that we will never have a Utopia in this life. We must consider ourselves as pilgrims passing through this land, looking for a better place (I Peter 2:11; Hebrews 11:16). To this end, the early saints sought comfort from earthly ills through the sacred Scriptures. Paul put it like this: "For whatsoever things were written aforetime [i.e., the Old Testament writings] were written for our learning, that through patience and through **comfort of the Scriptures** we might have hope" (Romans 15:4). It would be impossible to even estimate the multiplied times that fears have been allayed and spirits calmed by the comforting power of Heaven's Word.

The 23rd Psalm, for example, has been called the Nightingale Psalm because it sings sweetest at the midnight hour. In the course of my service to Christ, I have been called upon to conduct scores of funeral services. Occasionally, such requests come even from those who are scarcely religious at all. Significantly, however, I have never been asked to read select passages from Darwin's *Origin of the Species* or Tom Paine's *Age of Reason*. The literature of infidelity brings no ray of sunshine into the gloom of life's tragedies. Countless times, though, those crushed by death or other forms of disaster have drawn strength and courage from the ageless Volume.

CONCLUSION

Without question, there has never been a period within the past century when so many people have known so little about the Word of the Living God. Biblical ignorance is at an epidemic level, even among those who profess to be true followers of Christ. We simply must encourage more study of the divine Writings.

Christians should set aside a small nook within their homes as a refuge for daily study. Consideration should be given to the building of a good religious library, the access of which would greatly enhance one's understanding of numerous biblical subjects. One should discipline himself to regular periods of study and prayer. Preachers and teachers should be encouraged to bring us richer lessons which would challenge us to "dig deeper" into the treasures of the Word. Helpful portions of Scripture should be committed to memory. In short, we desperately need to become a people of the Book again.

There is much more to the Bible than simply reading it. Many folks read the Scriptures with some degree of regularity who have never really **studied** it. Study is work, and there is no quick, easy route to a ripe knowledge of the Bible. Solomon was correct when he said that "much study is a weariness of the flesh" (Ecclesiastes 12:12), but when that study is in the Revelation from Heaven, it is a happy weariness.

In the chapters to follow, we hope to make some study

recommendations which will excite you and motivate you to get into the fascinating world of Bible study with greater earnestness than you've ever had before. Absolutely nothing is more thrilling than a scholarly examination of Sacred Literature.

Questions on Chapter 1

1. List five ways in which God has made his presence known to man.

2. How does the law of "cause and effect" relate to the Bible? What are the only possible sources of the Bible's origin?

3. List seven things one has a right to expect of the Bible if it is, as it claims to be, the inspired Word of God.

4. Why is it important to have a correct view of one's origin?

5. According to Isaiah 43:7, for what purpose was man created? What is man's duty? Cite scripture.

6. What can one know about the character and mission of Jesus Christ apart from the New Testament record?

7. Explain how Jesus was able to resist yielding to Satan's temptations by the use of scripture.

8. Will God really condemn false teaching? How can one determine the difference between truth and error?

9. Why did the Sadducees not believe in the bodily resurrection from the dead?

10. How can the Scriptures assist us in times of distress and heartache?

Chapter 2

THE THEME OF THE BIBLE

The word "Bible" derives from the Greek term *biblos*. Originally, the word was used of the bark of the papyrus plant (from whence the first "paper" was manufactured), but finally came to mean simply "book." *Biblos* is the first word in the Greek New Testament, "The **book** of the generation of Jesus Christ...." The Bible is, therefore, the Book. Actually, though, the Bible is a whole library of books.

The Bible consists of sixty-six books; thirty-nine of these are in the Old Testament, and twenty-seven are in the New Testament. The entire sacred collection was penned over a span of some sixteen centuries by approximately forty different persons. Of the forty human authors used in writing the Scriptures, thirty-nine of them were Jews; the sole Gentile writer was Luke, author of two New Testament narratives.

As one approaches a study of the Bible, he should, in the very outset, have some concept of the general theme of this sacred volume. What is the Bible all about? Why was it given?

There are several ways that one can sum up the main thrust of the Holy Scriptures. The primary point of biblical emphasis is this—it concerns **the redemption of fallen man, by means of the mission of Christ, to the ultimate glory of God**. Another way of saying basically the same thing is this: the Bible is the record of man's **generation**, **degeneration**, and possible **regeneration** through the work of Jesus. Or again, the Bible record deals with: the preparation of Christ's advent to

Earth, the record of his earthly sojourn, and the promise of his return to judge the world. The fact of the matter is, as we shall presently observe, the whole of the sacred Scriptures is concerned, either directly or indirectly, with the mission and message of the Son of God.

HUMAN GENERATION

Why did God create man? This is a question that we cannot fully answer, for the Lord's purposes and ways are "unsearchable" and beyond our ability to analyze (Cf.: Romans 11:33). We may suggest, though, that it definitely was not because he **needed**, for some reason, to have us around. God, being infinite in all of his attributes (Cf.: Psalms 147:5), can, from the very nature of the case, stand in need of nothing! Since "love" is an essential part of Jehovah's being (I John 4: 8), we may assume that as an act of pure love, consistent with his sovereign will, humanity was brought into existence. Heavenly beings at the throne of God were constrained to exclaim, "....thou didst create all things, and **because of thy will** they were created" (Revelation 4:11). Though we doubtless have many unanswered questions about this matter, since it is a fact that we are "here," we must conclude that it is better "to be" than "not to be!"

MAN'S DEGENERATION

Of all the living creatures on earth, man was the solitary being made "in the image of God" (Genesis 1:26). Humanity was not fashioned in the **physical** image of deity, of course, for God is not physical (John 4:24; Luke 24:39; Matthew 16:17); rather, man was made in the spiritual, rational, and volitional image of God (Cf.: Ephesians 4:24). As a volitional creature, man is a being capable of making **choices** (Genesis

2:16, 17; Joshua 24:15; Isaiah 7:15; John 5:39, 40; 7:17; Revelation 22:17). Further, he was endowed with a responsibility to faithfully serve God (Ecclesiastes 12:13) and to glorify him (Isaiah 43:7). Unfortunately, finite man made some woefully evil choices, and so entered that unspiritual state called "sin."

The reality of sin is demonstrated in a number of different ways. (1) The Scriptures clearly teach it. "There is no man that sinneth not" (I Kings 8:46); indeed, "all have sinned" (Romans 3:23; cf.: I John 1:8, 10). (2) The conscience testifies to the presence of man's moral sensitivity, hence, his responsibility to a moral law (Romans 2:14, 15). No spiritually accountable individual has ever been free from the sense of personal guilt! (3) The witness of history underscores man's sense of sinfulness. The Roman philosopher Seneca said: "We have all sinned, some more, some less." A Chinese proverb declares: "There are two good men: one is dead and the other is not yet born!"

The reality of sin can also be seen in the horrible effects it has produced. Sin has affected man: (1) Physically—Disease and death were introduced into this world as a consequence of evil (Genesis 2:17; Romans 5:12). (2) Geophysically—Many of the erratic features of the earth's surface, which allow for storms, earthquakes, etc., are the result of the great Flood of Noah's day—which came as the effect of sin (Genesis 6:5ff). (3) Culturally—The communication problem that mankind has, due to the great variety of human languages, is traceable to ambitious rebellion on the part of our ancestors (Cf.: Genesis 11:1-9). (4) Psychologically—Man is generally without the peace of mind for which his heart longs [look at the number of psychiatrists listed in the Yellow Pages!]. "They have made them crooked paths; whosoever goeth therein doth not know peace" (Isaiah 59:8; cf.: 57:21). (5) Spiritually—By sin, man has created a chasm between himself and God. "Your iniquities have separated you and your God, and your sins have hid his face from you, so that he will not hear" (Isaiah

59:2). The ultimate "wages" of sinfulness is death, i.e., separation from God forever (Romans 6:23).

It is thus quite clear that sin is a past and present reality and that it has wrought havoc within the human family. All sensitive people want to know—"Is there a remedy?"

MAN'S REGENERATION

Here is an intriguing question: "Did God, before he created the first humans, know that they would sin?" The answer appears to be, "Yes," for inspiration informs us that the role of Christ in redemption was a part of the divine plan even "before the foundation of the world" (Ephesians 1:4; I Peter 1:20). If Jehovah knew that man would rebel, why then did he create him? We do not know, except to say that since whatever God does is right (Cf.: Genesis 18:25), his creation of beings of choice, hence, potential sinners, is not inconsistent with his holy nature. That aside, any seeming problem in this regard is negated by Heaven's offer of **pardon** to wicked humanity!

One cannot but wonder **why** God wanted to save this ungrateful creature who had so haughtily turned away from him. Well, here is an important truth—the Lord was not under **obligation** to do so! This seems apparent from the fact that angels sinned (II Peter 2:4; Jude 6), and yet, "not to angels doth he give help, but he giveth help to the seed of Abraham" (Hebrews 2:16). Rebellious angels seem to be without any redemptive plan! No wonder the psalmist wanted to know, "What is **man** that thou art mindful of him" (Psalms 8:4). We would still like to know!

A careful study of the Scriptures makes one thing absolutely clear—the Creator's efforts on behalf of sinful man are the result of **pure love.** Here are some facts that need to be carefully considered: (1) Jehovah's love for mankind was strictly **undeserved.** Salvation is offered to us even though we are ungodly, sinners, and enemies (note the use of those three

13

terms in Romans 5:6-10). "Herein is love, not that we loved God, but that he loved us...." (I John 4:10). (2) The love of God is **universal**, thus, not discriminatory (Cf.: John 3:15, 16). He would have all men to be saved (I Timothy 2:4)—if they **would be** saved (John 5:40), for he is not willing that any should perish (II Peter 3:9). (3) The Lord's love was not merely theoretical, rather, it was practical and **sacrificial**. Love **gives**, and so God gave his Son for the sin of the world. Moreover, the Son, with indentical love, gave himself as well (Galatians 1:4). (4) The love of deity is **unquenchable**. Nothing can separate us from the love of Christ. Read Romans 8:35ff and be thrilled by it. Only man's wanton rejection of that love can put him beyond the practical appropriation of the same!

GOD'S PLAN FOR HUMAN REGENERATION

The inspired Paul announced: "When the fulness of the time came, God sent forth his Son...." (Galatians 4:4). This remarkable passage reveals that Heaven's scheme of redemption was unfolded according to a precise program. It was meticulously designed so as to be most advantageous to human reception. Let us briefly consider this matter.

After the initial fall of man (Genesis 3), humankind progressively dredged itself deeper into wickedness. When more than a century of righteous preaching by the godly Noah produced little result, Jehovah sent the great Flood to purge the Earth (Genesis 6-8). From Noah, several generations later, the renowned Abraham was descended, and through him, the Hebrew nation was founded—from whom the Messiah eventually would come. Some four centuries after Abraham, the Lord through Moses, gave to the Hebrew family a **written revelation**, called the law of Moses. It was basically designed to accomplish three goals: (1) It **defined sin** and sharpened Israel's awareness of the same. To use Paul's expression, it made "sin exceeding sinful" (Romans 7:7, 13). (2) Additionally, the law

14

was designed to show man that he could never, by his own merit or effort, justify himself. The law thus emphasized man's need for a **Justifier**—for someone who would come and do for us that which we are unable to do for ourselves. (3) In harmony with that need, the Old Testament law, therefore, pointed the way to the coming Messiah. This was accomplished in a number of marvelous ways.

THE CHRIST OF THE OLD TESTAMENT

Jesus of Nazareth frequently and emphatically declared that he bore a vital relationship to the literature of the Old Testament. In the Sermon on the Mount, he said that he came to fulfil the law (Matthew 5:17). To some rebellious Jews, the Master once declared: "Ye search the scriptures, because ye think that in them ye have eternal life; and these are they which **bear witness of me**...." (John 5:39). Again, the Lord clearly affirmed: "....all things must needs be fulfilled, which are written in the law of Moses, and the prophets, and the psalms [a three-fold break-down of the Old Testament], **concerning me**" (Luke 24:44). In studying the Old Testament, therefore, it is imperative that the student realize that its basic message is a record of how God, in history, conditioned the world for the coming of his blessed Son.

The Old Testament prepared the human race for the coming of Jesus in several ways: First, there were the **theophanies**. These were temporary appearances of God in various forms (Cf.: Genesis 16:7ff; 18:1ff; 22:1ff, etc.). A careful consideration of all the facts can only lead to the conclusion that these manifestations were of the preincarnate (pre-human) Christ! Second, the Old Testament contains scores of **types** (i.e., a sort of pictorial preview) of the promised Lord. For instance, every bloody sacrifice was a symbol of that coming "Lamb of God that beareth away the sin of the world" (John 1:29). Finally, in more than three hundred **prophecies**, containing countless minute details, the first advent of Jesus was graphically made known.

REDEMPTION CENTERED IN THE DEATH OF CHRIST

No one who studies the Bible for long can be unaware of the fact that the entire sacred record is centered in the **death and resurrection** of Jesus Christ. But this question intrigues us: **why** did God's Son have to die? Was there no other way in which Jehovah could deal with the sin-problem? Obviously not! Surely our Father did not choose the death of his Son as a whimsical option! There are several important truths that must be considered here.

First, the Bible forcefully affirms that our great Maker is an absolutely **holy** Being (Cf.: Isaiah 6:3; Revelation 4:8), and as such, he simply cannot ignore sin. The prophet Habakkuk expressed it like this: "Your eyes are too pure to look on evil; you cannot tolerate wrong" (1:13a). But in the second place, another of the Lord's attributes is his perfect justice. Righteousness and justice are the very foundation of his throne (Psalms 89:14). In view of these facts, namely that God is both holy and just, the irresistable truth is this—**sin must be punished!**

Now if the Almighty were a cold, totally vengeful God [as infidelity has frequently characterized him], he could simply banish man from his divine presence forever and that would settle the matter. But the truth is, he is not that kind of God! Our Creator is loving (I John 4:8) and he is "rich in mercy" (Ephesians 2:4). Here, then, is the problem—how does a loving, merciful God pardon wickedly rebellious man, and, at the same time, preserve his holy justice? The answer to the puzzle is : CHRIST!

Paul addresses this very issue in the third chapter of the book of Romans. How can God be just, and yet a justifier of sinful man? Jehovah is able to extend his grace [favor] on the basis of the redemptive life and death of his Son, Jesus Christ (3:24ff). Here is how the heavenly plan was implemented. As an eternal divine Being, the personal Word [Grk. *Logos*] took upon himself the form of a man. He came to the Earth as a human being (John 1:1-4; 14; Philemon 2:5-11; I Timothy 3:16). Christ thus fully shared our nature and the human experience. He was even tempted in all points just as we are, yet here was the difference—he never yielded to temptation, and so, never sinned (Hebrews 4:15).

But what has this to do with us? Simply this—since Christ was a tested person (Cf.: Isaiah 28:16), and so, found perfect (II Corinthians 5:21; I Peter 2:22), the Father **allowed him to stand in for us**, i.e., to take our place, to receive our punishment. Isaiah summarizes it as follows: "He was wounded for our transgressions, he was bruised for our iniquities; the chastisement of our peace was upon him; and with his stripes we are healed. All we like sheep have gone astray; we have turned every one to his own way; and Jehovah hath laid on him the iniquity of us all" (53:5, 6). Christ thus became a **substitutionary** sacrifice, paying the price for human salvation.

In the gift of Christ, Heaven's mercy is extended; in the death of the Lord, divine justice is satisfied; in the resurrection of Jesus, God's plan is historically documented!

After the Gospel Accounts (Matthew, Mark, Luke, and John) carefully document the historical facts of Christ's death, his burial, and his triumphant resurrection from the grave, the balance of the New Testament record guides the honest mind into the knowledge of how this wonderful plan can be accommodated to the human need. The book of Acts reveals how men and women of the first century appropriated Heaven's blessings of salvation to their personal needs. In obedience to the Lord's plan of redemption (John 3:36 ASV; Galatians 5:6; Hebrews 5:9; Acts 2:38), sincere souls became Christians (Cf.: Acts 11:26; I Peter 4:16), and the church of Christ spread like a burning flame across the antique world. The balance of the New Testament also shows how one is to spiritually mature "in the Lord" (Cf.: II Peter 3:18).

THE FINAL EMPHASIS

A major concluding emphasis of the biblical record is the promise of the return of Christ to judge the world and to gather his own people unto himself in everlasting glory. No consideration of the Bible's theme would be complete without mention of this important truth.

Christ himself prophesied that he would literally come again (Matthew 25:31; John 14:3). His coming was to be: personal (I Thessalonians 4:16); visible (Acts 1:11); sudden and unexpected (I Thessalonians 5:2,3); glorious (Matthew 25:31); victorious (II Thessalonians 1:7-10); and terminal, i.e., a consummation of earthly affairs (I Corinthians 15:24). In a word, it may be said that the **entire purpose of the Bible** is to prepare the human race for this day!

A FINAL COMMENT

No detailed, analytical study of the Scriptures will be profitable unless the student at least has a general impression of the foregoing thrust of the divine Book. The Bible is principally a book of SALVATION. It's history, geography, biography, theology, etc. must be viewed in this light. As we approach this awesome task, let us "take off our shoes" (Cf.: Exodus 3:5), for we are treading on holy ground.

Questions on Chapter 2

1. What is the origin of the word "Bible?"

2. How many books in the Bible? In the O.T.? In the N.T.?

3. What is the primary purpose of the Bible?

4. Why was man created, and in what sense was he created in the image of God?

5. List five ways sin has affected the human family.

6. What was the purpose of Jehovah's selection and separation of the Hebrew nation? Who was the first "Hebrew"?

7. What was the first written revelation from God to man?

8. How does the Old Testament relate to Christ?

9. What is a "theophany"?

10. Why did Christ have to die?

Chapter 3

PRINCIPLES OF BIBLE INTERPRETATION

In the final epistle he wrote before being executed for the cause of Jesus Christ, the apostle Paul, to Timothy, admonished: "Give diligence to present thyself approved unto God, a workman that needeth not to be ashamed, handling aright the word of truth" (II Timothy 2:15). The expression "handling aright" (ASV) translates the Greek word *orthotomeo*, from *orthos* ("straight") and *temno* ("to cut"), hence, to cut straight. Within this context the term simply means to **teach accurately, soundly**. The emphasis is the exact opposite of that disposition described by the same writer in II Corinthians 4:2 as "handling the word of God deceitfully," which suggests corrupting it with error. What an awesome responsibility it is to teach the message of Jehovah God!

The Bible is filled with warnings about the proper approach to the sacred Scriptures. For instance, Paul wrote of those who would "pervert [i.e., turn into that of opposite character] the gospel of Christ" (Galatians 1:7), and Peter spoke of those ignorant and unsteadfast persons who "wrest" [i.e., twist] the Scriptures unto their own destruction (II Peter 3:16).

The Word of God has been "settled in heaven" (Psalms 119:89), and it is not, therefore, to be supplemented, diminished, nor altered in any way (Cf.: Deuteronomy 4:2; 12:32; Proverbs 30:6; Revelation 22:18, 19).

It is possible for one to have a large portion of the Scriptures in his mind, and yet, have it so confused, that he misrepresents the true message of God. The Jews were constantly searching the Old Testament writings (Cf.: John 5:39), yet most of them neither recognized nor accepted the Messiah because, as Paul later comments, a veil of preconception shrouded their hearts when the Law was read (II Corinthians 3:14, 15). How very cautious, therefore, ought we to be in our approach to, and presentation of, the Holy Bible.

How can the sincere student of the sacred Oracles cultivate his skills so that he may be confident of a correct handling of the Truth? We would suggest the following principles which are quite essential if one is to have an accurate approach to Bible study.

(1) **Recognize the nature of the document with which you are dealing**. The attitude that one has toward the Bible is of paramount importance. If one feels that he is dealing with a book that is an admixture of the human and the divine, so that only that which really "turns him on" is the **word of God** (a common modernistic allegation), he will not have that degree of reverence that enhances sound interpretation. The Bible is the verbally inspired word of God (II Timothy 3:16, 17), and one must approach it with the attitude, "This is God speaking to me. I am bound to listen."

(2) **Realize that the Bible was meant to be understood**. The notion must be discarded that the Scriptures are an antique, inexplicable riddle; rather, one must know that the Lord intended his will to be comprehended. "Wherefore be ye not foolish, but understand what the will of the Lord is" (Ephesians 5:17). Paul told the brothers at Ephesus that "when ye read [that which the apostle had written], ye can perceive my understanding in the mystery of Christ" (Ephesians 3:4). The term "mystery" does not imply that God's will is "mysterious," only that in former ages, prior to the Christian era, it had not fully been made known. Paul is suggesting that **now** it has been revealed, however, and one can read and appreciate it (Cf.: 3:5). We can, and we must, **know** the truth if we are to

be set free from sin (John 8:32), and that truth is the word of God (John 17:17). The Scriptures are not the exclusive property of some clergyhood, to be doled out and accepted, without personal investigation, by the public. Each man is responsible before Jehovah to examine the inspired documents personally. "Now these were more noble than those in Thessalonica, in that they perceived the word with all readiness of mind, examining the scriptures daily, whether these things were so" (Acts 17:11).

(3) **Be aware of the different covenants of the Bible**. One must be able to distinguish between the different covenant periods of biblical history. In various ages of the past, the Lord made different covenants with individuals and with nations, and no one can understand his duty to the Creator without knowing to which covenant system he is responsible. Abraham was not required to build an ark, as was Noah, for God's covenants with the two men were different. Abraham was never obligated to observe the Passover, for the Passover was part of a law-system that came years later. Joshua was never commanded to "be baptized" for the forgiveness of his sins, for that requirement was part of a later law, the New Testament system. John the Baptizer never observed the "Lord's supper" on Sunday, for the communion supper is a feature of the kingdom [church] of Christ (Luke 22:29, 30), and John died before the church was established.

One of the greatest errors of the religious world is the failure to recognize that the Law of Moses was a temporary system, designed to escort the Jewish nation to Christ (Galatians 3:24, 25), and with that task accomplished, it was abolished (Ephesians 2:15; Colossians 2:14). Men are thus not amenable to that law today. That is why Christians do not offer animal sacrifices to God (as the Hebrews did under the Mosaic economy), burn incense as a worship ritual, observe the sabbath as a holy day, have a special "priesthood" though whom God must be approached, etc. These things were elements of a covenant-system that has long since been replaced by a better system (Cf.: Hebrews 7:22; 8:6).

(4) **Discernment between different types of narratives**. A correct understanding of the Bible demands that one discriminate between the various forms of language in the sacred text. There are historical narratives, prophecies, poetry sections, etc. Many mistakes have been made by a failure to recognize this fact. For instance, religious modernism suggests that the first two chapters of Genesis are some sort of ancient poem that is not to be pressed as real history (such a view is designed to accommodate the biblical record to the gross assumptions of evolution), but the **style** of the narrative is **historical prose**, just as the balance of the book of Genesis is! On the other hand, materialists—those who contend that man is wholly mortal and thus at death the wicked will be totally exterminated—will dip into the poetic sections of the Bible, such as Job, Psalms, etc., and attempt to argue that rebellious man is annihilated when he dies. When Job affirmed that "he that goeth down to Sheol shall come up no more" (7:9), that was simply his way of saying that once a man dies, he does not return to his old, earthly routine anymore; he comes back to "his house" no more (vs. 10). It is very wrong to press this poetry into a doctrinal argument.

Too, one must recognize the difference between "literal" language and "figurative" language in the Bible. The creation "days" of Genesis 1 are not figures of speech indicating vast ages of time, as theistic evolutionists allege. Both the context of Genesis 1, as well as the companion text of Exodus 20:8-11, clearly forbid this bizarre notion. In this latter context, the creation "days" are the same type of "day" as the Hebrew sabbath! On the other hand, it is quite dangerous to literalize passages that are obviously figurative. Christ once said that some make themselves "eunuchs for the kingdom of heaven's sake" (Matthew 19:12). Origin, a writer of the post-apostolic age, apparently interpreted the Lord's symbolic statement **literally** and so castrated himself—a rather high price to pay for misunderstanding the nature of the language! A very common error of the premillennialists (those who believe that Christ will return to reign on earth for 1,000 years) is an attempt to literalize certain portions of the Bible that are obviously symbolic. For example, the beautiful symbolism of the wolf dwelling with the lamb (Isaiah 11:6ff) does not point to a future earthly condition among animals; rather, it is a figurative description of the peace between those nations that flow into the house of God (Isaiah 2:2-4) in the **gospel age**, as indeed Paul reveals by his use of Isaiah's prophecy in Romans 15:8-12.

One must study to learn the identifying traits of certain types of literature and language as he commences his investigation of the Bible. There are several good books available for the serious student and these will be mentioned in a later chapter of this volume.

(5) **Distinguish between the permanent and the temporary**. Some things in the Bible were designed by Jehovah to be age-lasting, that is, they are to abide co-extensive with the Christian era. Other elements were intended to serve in a specific capacity, temporary in nature, and so, when their purpose was realized, they passed away. A failure to recognize this truth has led to some enormous errors.

For example, some ultra-dispensationalists argue that water baptism (e.g., in Acts 8:36ff; 10:47, 48) was but a **Jewish ceremonial ritual**, hence, such passed away with the abrogation of Moses' Law (which, they contend, was divinely operative until the end of the book of Acts!). Such, though, is a false idea, for the water baptism of the new birth (Cf.: John 3:5, Ephesians 5:26) was designed to last to the end of the Christian age (Cf.: Matthew 28:18-20).

On the other hand, "Pentecostalism" fails to see that the miraculous gifts of the first century were intended to document the **divine source** of the inspired messages of those whom God selected to be instruments of his revelatory process. Hence, those gifts were **temporarily** bestowed until such a time as that need was fulfilled. Accordingly, miraculous gifts were not ordained as a permanent endowment of the church (Cf.: I Corinthians 13:8ff; Ephesians 4:8ff), and they are not available today.

(6) **Separate custom from principle**. Unless one believes that the Bible fell directly from heaven in its present form (which it did not), he must deal with the presence of certain cultural elements in the divine record. How does the Bible student distinguish between **custom** and **principle**? When some religious groups practice feet-washing as an act of religious devotion, appealing to John 13:4ff, they fail to understand that the washing of feet had been a common practice among the sandal-wearing Jews for centuries. It was a servant's function to wash the feet of guests. This relation is depicted in the Old Testament. "Behold, thy handmaid is a servant to wash the feet of the servants of my Lord" (I Samuel 25:41). The Master Teacher, therefore, used this cultural situation to teach his disciples, who had been arguing among themselves about who would be the greatest (Luke 22:24ff), that the path to greatness was by way of **service**. There is nothing in John 13 to indicate that the literal practice of feet-washing was to be bound upon the Lord's people as an age-lasting requirement.

By way of contrast, though, when Scottish commentator William Barclay declares that the instruction of I Timothy 2, limiting woman's teaching sphere (see verse 12 especially), is a mere "temporary" regulation laid down to meet a cultural situation [*Letters to Timothy, Titus, Philemon*, pp. 78, 79], he errs exceedingly, for the apostle Paul, within this context, grounds his argumentation upon: (a) the sexual distinctions between man and woman that go back to the very creation; and, (b) man and woman's respective roles in the original fall. The apostolic injunction is based upon **timeless principle** and not **temporary custom**.

Similarly, Christ's teaching regarding marriage and divorce (Matthew 19:4ff) is anchored in principles for the home established by God in the beginning. It must be stressed that "creation" ordinances are indicators of trans-cultural princi-

25

ples (Cf.: I Corinthians 11:2-16; Ephesians 5:23ff).

(7) **Understand the difference between the circumstantial and the spiritual**. A man once boasted to this writer that he had been baptized in the Jordan River, as though that made his immersion somehow more valid than that administered in a baptistry. But the Lord's baptism in Jordan was a mere incidental circumstance. Others declare that the baptismal **form** (immersion, sprinkling) is unimportant. They overlook, though, the **spiritual picture** that immersion conveys—the burial and resurrection of Jesus Christ (Romans 6:3, 4; Colossians 2:12). The basis of the command is thus not circumstantial.

The matter of whether the Lord's supper is observed on an upper floor or at ground level is inconsequential—mere circumstance is involved in the biblical instances (Mark 14:15; Acts 20:8). But the **components** of the communion—bread and fruit of the vine (Matthew 26:26-29), which symbolize the Lord's body and blood, are **spiritual**, and so, are not to be altered. Also, the supper observance on each first day of the week (Acts 20:7; cf.: I Corinthians 16:2—Greek text), which points to Christ's resurrection day, has a spiritual basis and is, therefore, bound upon the Christian.

(8) **Respect the context**. Biblical contexts are of two kinds—the near and the remote. The near context is the textual information that precedes and follows the verse under consideration. The remote context is additional material, relating to the same subject, elsewhere in the Bible. Many Bible passages are horribly perverted because context has been ignored.

Some preachers apparently think that the promise, "....be not anxious how or what ye shall speak: for it will be given you in that hour...." (Matthew 10:19), was made for them, for their lessons evidence little forethought! But the context reveals that the **miraculously endowed** disciples were in view. The prohibition, "Handle not, nor taste, nor touch" (Colossians 2:21) has provided fodder for many a temperance sermon; actually, though, the passage relates to "the precepts

26

and doctrines of men" (2:22). Paul's advice concerning marital celibacy (I Corinthians 7:1, 7, 8, etc.) is contextually qualified by his allusion to "the distress [i.e., persecution] that is upon us" (Cf.: 7:26, 28, 29, 35, 40).

John the Baptizer once stated: "....he [Jesus] shall baptize you in the Holy Spirit and in fire" (Matthew 3:11). This passage is often misunderstood because contextual details, both immediate and remote, are not considered. First, the narrative is a **summary** of the preaching ministry of John over a period of time. The imperfect tense verb "went out" (3:5) implies a steady stream of listeners; it thus involves a variety of people—good and bad. Second, the immediate context indicates that the baptism of "fire" is the ultimate punishment of the wicked (Cf.: 3:10,12). Third, the remote context reveals that the baptism "in the Spirit" referred to the Lord's apostles (Acts 1:2, 5, 26; 2:4), and not to the public in general. Context is crucial!

Again, some read Romans 5:1—"Being therefore justified by faith...."—and assume that salvation is by "faith alone." But they have ignored the broader biblical context in which additional conditions of redemption are included (Cf.: Acts 17: 30; 2:38; Romans 10:10). And so, context is vitally important. A text, out of context, is a mere pretext!

(9) **Let the Bible explain itself.** The Bible is its own best commentary, and a comparison of parallel words or phrases and historical or doctrinal statements, which may be difficult to understand in one setting, can frequently be cleared up by a corresponding passage elsewhere.

For instance, Christ declared: "If any man cometh unto me, and hateth not his own father, and mother, and wife, and children, and brethren, and sisters, yea, and his own life also, he cannot be my disciple" (Luke 14:26). How is one to explain such a seemingly harsh requirement? A comparison with the parallel statement in Matthew's gospel solves the difficulty. That narrative reads: "He that loveth father or mother more than me is not worthy of me; and he that loveth son or daughter more than me is not worthy of me" (Matthew 10:37). Jesus thus did not teach that one must literally hate his dear ones; rather, he was suggesting that love for **Him** must be supreme! He will take second place to none! What a marvelous evidence of his deity!

In John 3:16 we are informed that those who "believe" on Christ should not perish, but have eternal life. Some would interpret the belief of this passage as mere mental "trust" in the Lord. On the other hand, Hebrews 5:9 affirms that Christ is the author of eternal salvation to such as "obey" him. Note how a comparison of the two passages makes clear the nature of belief.

John 3:16—he that believes----------------- hath eternal life
Hebrews 5:9—he that obeys------------- hath eternal salvation

It is quite clear that the belief of John 3:16 is an **obedient** belief, and not a mere mental exercise. It is an "obedience of faith" (Cf.: Romans 1:5; 16:26).

(10) **Always maintain an honest heart.** The conscientious Bible student should diligently pursue the following guidelines: (a) Give yourself to a thorough study of the Word, but never be afraid to admit, "I do not know," when such is the case. Do not, out of pride, attempt to bluff answers that you don't have. (b) As much as possible, be an independent student. Yes, respectfully study the research and writings of others, but do not be intimidated by them. Even the ripest Bible scholars can sometimes be wrong. Yet, don't hesitate to ask for help from faithful Christians who may have more experience in Bible study than you do. (c) Do not attempt to conjure up novel and bizarre teachings for the purpose of attracting attention or gaining a following. You might be surprised at how many have done such things. (d) Never hesitate to admit that you have been in error, and modify your views when convicted by biblical evidence. (e) Pray to God for the wisdom to deal responsibly with his Word, and then, boldly and compassionately teach to others what you have learned. Knowledge retained only condemns!

Questions on Chapter 3

1. What does it mean to "handle aright" the word of truth?

2. Why did most Jews not recognize Jesus as the Messiah?

3. Comment upon this statement: "The Bible is a confusing book. No one can really understand it."

4. Will Abraham be lost because he was not baptized? Explain your answer.

5. Does Job 7:9 teach that the dead will not be raised? Explain the fallacy of materialism in this connection.

6. What was the purpose of miracles in the 1st century? What passages show that miraculous signs were not a permanent endowment for the church?

7. If a biblical teaching is grounded upon fundamental historical facts, relating to creation, the fall, etc., would it be a temporary or permanent obligation?

8. If Christians are obligated to eat "bread" and drink the "fruit of the vine" in the observance of the Lord's supper, why ought they not also meet for that communion in an "upper room?"

9. In studying a passage of scripture, it is very important to respect the _____, for a _____ out of _____ is a mere _____.

10. How can one demonstrate that John 3:16 does not teach that salvation is by faith alone, without other acts of obedience?

Chapter 4

PERIODS OF BIBLE HISTORY

There are many people who have accumulated numerous "bits and pieces" of Bible knowledge, but they have never learned to put it together, particularly in its chronological sequence. They know, for example, that Moses led the children of Israel out of Egypt into freedom, and also that Solomon was a great and wise king of Israel, but which of these men lived first? Many haven't the remotest idea. Was Samson, the renowned strong man of the Bible, a slave in Egypt? A king in Israel? Both? Or Neither? When did he live? What role did he play in Israel's history? These questions, and hundreds of others considerably more complex, make it absolutely imperative that the serious Bible student learn the great periods of Scripture history.

For our own study purposes in this chapter, we are dividing the entire Bible into **eleven** historical periods. It is necessary, first of all, that the student **memorize** the titles of these eleven ages. Go over these several times each day for a week or more, until you know them forwards and backwards. This is extremely important since, in the remainder of the chapter, we will put some "meat" on the bones of this brief outline. Here are the eleven periods—get to work on them!

1. The Period of Beginnings
2. The Hebrew Family
3. The Egyptian Bondage

4. The Wilderness Wandering
5. The Conquest and Settlement of Canaan
6. The United Kingdom
7. The Divided Kingdom
8. The Babylonian Captivity and Restoration
9. The Inter-biblical Period
10. The Life of Christ
11. The Establishment and Expansion of Christianity

A SKETCH OF THE PERIODS OF BIBLE HISTORY

After one has memorized the names of these periods of Bible history, he is ready to begin looking at these eras in greater detail. He should focus upon the major events of each period, committing the basic facts to memory. It will be helpful to test oneself (or work with a companion) over and over on these points, for "repetition is the mother of learning."

The Period of Beginnings—The first eleven chapters of the Book of Genesis have been appropriately called the "Period of Beginnings," because they are concerned with the "beginnings" of so many different things (a number of these will be discussed in a later chapter). Primarily, though, we will list four significant events that occurred in this period of history.

First, there is the **creation** record (Genesis 1, 2). This is the sacred account of the six days of divine activity in which the entire universe, with all living creature-kinds—including man—were brought into existence. The creation account, incidentally, cannot, in any way, be harmonized with the theory of evolution. Second, there is the **fall of humanity**. The early Genesis record reveals that though man was created upright (Cf.: Ecclesiastes 7:29), through the freedom of choice that was given him (Cf.: Joshua 24:15), he sinned and so departed from his holy estate, thereby introducing sin and death (Romans 5:12). Third, there is the narrative concerning **the universal Flood**. As the human race grew, and became domi-

31

nated by rebellion against the Creator, Jehovah, as an act of divine justice, destroyed the entire ancient world, with the exception of the inmates of Noah's ark (Genesis 6-8; I Peter 3:20). Fourth, there was the **multiplication of human languages**. The society of the ancient post-flood world refused to heed Jehovah's command to disperse. Accordingly, the Lord confused their language and so "scattered them abroad" upon the face of the earth (Genesis 11:1-9).

The Hebrew Family—Commencing with Genesis 12, God selects Abram (later called Abraham) to be the head of a new race. Abraham is the first person in the Bible to be called a "Hebrew" (Genesis 14:13). Through Abraham and his "seed" ultimately the Christ would come (Genesis 12:3; 22:18; Galatians 3:16). Genesis 12-50 is thus basically the account of how the Lord was preparing the world for the coming of his Son through the lives of four men: Abraham, Isaac, Jacob, and Joseph. From the time that Jehovah led Abraham into Canaan, until Jacob and his children migrated down into Egypt, about 215 years lapsed (Cf.: Genesis 12:4; 21:5; 25:26; 47:9).

In this connection it is important to observe that the selection of Canaan (Palestine) as a home for the Hebrews is quite significant. Canaan was the most ideal spot on earth (trade routes from all points passing through her borders) for the influencing of great world powers in preparation for the coming Messiah!

The Egyptian Bondage—The Book of Exodus begins with Jacob and his family going down into Egypt for relief from a famine in Canaan. Years earlier, Joseph, Jacob's son, had been sold into Egyptian slavery by his jealous brothers (Cf.: Acts 7:9). Due to the providential working of God (Cf.: Genesis 45:5ff), however, Joseph became a powerful ruler in Egypt. Eventually, the older patriarchs died but the Israelites were fruitful and increased in number and "the land was filled with them." Presently, however, a ruler came to the throne "who knew not Joseph" (Exodus 1:8) and the Hebrews were made slaves in Egypt. Thus was begun a period of history known as the Egyptian Bondage.

Scholars are disagreed as to how much time was actually involved in the bondage period. Some passages (e.g., Exodus 12:40) seem to indicate that is was 430 years (though the Septuagint [Greek translation of the O.T.] and the Samaritan Pentateuch include the patriarchs' sojourn in Canaan in this figure). Others contend, however, that the bondage period was only some 215 years. Their conclusions are based upon Paul's statement in Galatians 3:16, 17 that from the "promise" to the "law" was 430 years.

As the Israelites were learning many valuable lessons in the bondage era, Moses was being trained by the Lord to be their great deliverer. Eighty years of the great prophet's life were spent during this epoch of history (forty in the courts of Egypt and forty in the wilderness of Midian).

In the wilderness of Sinai, Jehovah spoke to Moses and commissioned him to go and deliver Israel from their bondage. The Lord visited a series of ten devastating plagues upon the Egyptians in order to convince Pharaoh to release the Hebrews. Actually, the plagues were direct attacks on the "gods" of Egypt thus demonstrating that the God of the Hebrews was the true deity (Cf.: Exodus 7:16, 17). By a mighty hand did Jehovah thus deliver Israel from bondage (Cf.: Exodus 14).

The Wilderness Wandering—The Israelites crossed the Red Sea and entered the Sinaitic peninsula; journeying southward, they came to the mountains of Horeb. Here they encamped for about a year with the following events transpiring: (1) The Law of Moses was given (Exodus 19-31). (2) Israel worshipped the golden calf and punishment was rendered unto them (Exodus 32). (3) The Tabernacle (a temporary worship facility) was constructed and consecrated (Exodus 35-40). (4) The nation was numbered and organized (Numbers 1-2). It is believed that the entire nation numbered more than two million people.

The Hebrews then traveled northward to Kadesh-barnea, from whence twelve spies were dispatched to survey the land of Canaan. Ten of the twelve (Joshua and Caleb excepted) returned with such a faithless report that Jehovah decreed that the nation would not enter the Promised Land until the present generation had expired in the wilderness (Numbers 13, 14). Because of an act of disobedience, not even Moses would be allowed to enter the land (Cf.: Numbers 20:1-13). Israel wandered in the wilderness of Sinai for forty years (a year for each day the scouts had spied out the land—Numbers 14:34); here they learned numerous lessons about the power of Jehovah and the need to depend absolutely upon him.

Conquest and Settlement of Canaan—After conquering three regions east of the Jordan (Gilead, Bashan, and Midian—Numbers 21, 25, 31), the Israelites crossed the River and entered the promised land. The rite of circumcision, which had been neglected in the wilderness, was performed and the Passover, commemorating their deliverance from Egypt, was observed (Joshua 5). The Hebrews then substantially conquered the land of Canaan. Their plan of conquest was essentially threefold: First, they invaded the central section including such cities as Jericho and Ai (Joshua 3-8). Second, they turned southward and defeated a confederation of Canaanite kings. During this campaign, the famous battle of "Joshua's long day" occurred (Joshua 10). Third, Israels's army then marched northward defeating several independent military leaders (Joshua 11). This ended the active invasion of the Canaan and "the land rested from war" (11:23). The conquest had taken about seven years (Cf.: Joshua 14:10). It must be noted, however, that while the conquest was considered to be essentially complete, many local pockets of resistance still prevailed, and were **tolerated** by the Hebrews—a fact that wrought sad consequences in the following years!

Additionally, it should be observed that Palestine was divided among the tribes of Israel into territorial regions (Numbers 32; Joshua 15-17; Joshua 18, 19), the Levites receiving no land portion; rather, they were assigned forty-eight cities.

From the time of Joshua, until Saul, the first king of

Israel, the Hebrews were governed by a series of leaders called "Judges." Most of them ruled over a limited territory and sometimes they were leading simultaneously; at other times, no judge was in power. This era has been called the "Dark Ages" of Hebrew history because of the apostasy that was so characteristic of it. A familiar refrain in the Book of Judges is this: "And every man did that which was right in his own eyes" (Cf.: 17:6; 21:25). This period of history, of more than three and one half centuries (Cf.: I Kings 6:1), was characterized by four cycles: (a) The people would rebel against Jehovah; (b) The Lord would send an oppressor to punish them; (c) Israel would cry out for deliverance; and, (d) God would raise up a judge to overthrow the enemy and free his people.

The United Kingdom—The last great leader in the "judges" era was Samuel, who was actually a judge, prophet, and priest. During the latter days of Samuel's administration, Israel pled with the prophet for a "king," so that they might be "like all the nations" (I Samuel 8:5, 19, 20). Though the request displeased the Lord (I Samuel 8:7, 8; cf.: Hosea 13:11), nonetheless their petition was answered (that they might taste the fruit of their rebellion) and a king was appointed for them.

The first of Israel's kings was **Saul**, a farm boy (I Samuel 11:5) from the tribe of Benjamin (Cf.: I Samuel 11; 13-15; 17-25; 31). According to the New Testament, his reign was forty years long (Acts 13:21), though some scholars think this may have included the tenure of his son (Cf.: II Samuel 2:10). Saul led the Hebrew nation in a number of mighty military efforts against their pagan neighbors. Sadly, however, he became unfaithful to Jehovah (Cf.: I Samuel 13; 15) and died in disgrace (II Samuel 1:19, 24).

Israel's greatest king was the popular and courageous **David** (I Samuel 19-31; II Samuel 1-24; I Kings 1-2; I Chronicles 10-29). For the first seven years of his reign, only the tribe of Judah acknowledged David as king (the other tribes submitting to Ishbosheth, Saul's son; cf.: II Samuel 5:5); after that, however, the nation united under the famous monarch.

David reigned for a total of forty years (II Samuel 5:4). He captured the old Canaanite city of Jebus (Jerusalem) and made it ihis capital. He longed to build a temple for Jehovah there, but since he was a man of war, the Lord did not permit him to accomplish this task (I Chronicles 22:8). As a military leader, David was quite successful, conquering many of the surrounding tribes (II Samuel 8:1-13).

Though David was a "man after God's own heart," he, nonetheless, was occasionally weak. His great sin with the beautiful Bathsheba is well known (II Samuel 11, 12), and even though he repented of that wickedness (Cf.: Psalms 51), he suffered great domestic heartaches as a consequence of it (II Samuel 12:10ff). In spite of his weakness, David was a great ruler and Jehovah promised him that from his seed the Messiah would come (II Samuel 7:12, 13).

David's heir to the throne was his son, **Solomon** (I Kings 1-11; II Chronicles 1-9), who extended the borders of the Israelite kingdom from Mesopotamia in the east to Egypt in the west (I Kings 4:21)—a region of some 50,000 square miles. Solomon was a master builder; he built the great temple in Jerusalem, and, in addition, a marvelous palace. He also constructed many store cities and carried on immense trade enterprises. It has been estimated that his income may have exceeded one hundred million dollars annually!

Sadly, though, the latter years of Solomon's forty year reign (Cf.: II Chronicles 9:30) were marred by apostasy. His many marriages to pagan women resulted in his turning his heart away from Jehovah God (I Kings 11:4) and this spiritual decay, which involved actual idolatry, was a direct contributor to the ultimate division of the nation.

The Divided Kingdom—Though the seeds of national division had long been working among the Lord's people (Cf.: Judges 8:1-3; 12:1-6; II Samuel 2:9, 10; 19:42, 43), the actual split came in the days of Rehoboam, Solomon's son. Rehoboam was an extremely foolish leader. Following the advice of his boyhood companions, he threatened to increase the burdens of the nation, and so, there was national rebellion (I Kings 12:19).

Ten of the twelve Hebrew tribes became known as the northern **Kingdom of Israel** (Cf.: I Kings 12 to II Kings 17). The new king of Israel was Jeroboam, who made drastic changes in the worship system of Jehovah (Cf.: I Kings 12:25ff). He altered the **object** of worship (from Jehovah to golden calves), the **place** of worship (from Jerusalem to Bethel and Dan), the **time** of the feast day (from the 7th to the 8th month), and the **priesthood** (from the tribe of Levi to any tribe). Some twenty-one times the inspired record mentions that "he made Israel to sin." The northern kingdom lasted for about 210 years (931/30 B.C. to 722/21 B.C.) and it was ruled over by nineteen different kings. Though a number of prophets, e.g., Elijah, Elisha, Amos, Hosea, tried to call Israel to repentance, the rebellious nation dredged itself deeper and deeper into idolatrous apostasy. Finally, Jehovah brought the Assyrian nation against Israel. There was a deportation of Hebrews into Assyria in 734 B.C. under Tiglath-pileser (II Kings 15:29; 16:7-9) and again in 722 B.C. under Shalmaneser/Sargon. According to Assyrian records, some 27,290 people of Israel were taken captive. Many, however, were left in the land where they intermingled with colonists from Assyria. The expression "Ten Lost Tribes" is thus somewhat of a misnomer.

The southern kingdom, known as the **Kingdom of Judah**, was composed of the tribes of Judah and Benjamin (I Kings 12:21), as well as some Levites and others from Israel who "set their hearts to seek Jehovah" (II Chronicles 11:13-16). This kingdom existed for some 325 years (931 B.C.—606 B.C.), or until the time of the Babylonian Captivity. The southern kingdom had twenty kings, and though a few of these (e.g., Hezekiah, Josiah) attempted reforms, the nation became increasingly involved in idolatry, and so, according to God's plan, they were removed as captives into Babylon for a period of seventy years.

THE KINGS OF ISRAEL AND JUDAH

Israel		Judah	
Jeroboam I	22 years	Rehoboam	17 years
Nadab	2 years	Abijah	3 years
Baasha	24 years	Asa	41 years
Elah	2 years	Jehoshaphat	25 years
Zimri	7 days	Jehoram	8 years
Omri	12 years	Ahaziah	1 year
Ahab	22 years	Athaliah	6 years
Ahaziah	2 years	Joash	40 years
Jehoram	12 years	Amaziah	29 years
Jehu	28 years	Uzziah	52 years
Jehoahaz	17 years	Jotham	16 years
Jehoash	16 years	Ahaz	16 years
Jeroboam II	41 years	Hezekiah	29 years
Zachariah	6 months	Manasseh	55 years
Shallum	1 month	Amon	2 years
Menahem	10 years	Josiah	31 years
Pekahiah	2 years	Jehoahaz	3 months
Pekah	20 years	Jehoiakim	11 years
Hoshea	9 years	Jehoiachin	3 months
		Zedekiah	11 years

The Babylonian Captivity and Restoration—Due to Judah's idolatrous practices and moral wickedness, the prophets declared that Jehovah would "raise up the Chaldeans [Babylonians]" (Cf.: Habakkuk 1:6) who would march against them and take them captive. The prophet Jeremiah had warned that the land of Israel would be made desolate and the captives would "serve the king of Babylon seventy years" (Jeremiah 25:11). The captivity was mainly accomplished in three deportations: (1) There was a "princely" exile in 606/05 B.C., when such men as Daniel, Shadrach, Meshach, and Abednego were taken away (II Chronicles 36:6, 7; Daniel 1:1-3). (2)

38

There was the exile of the "upper class" in 597 B.C. (II Kings 24:14, 18). (3) There was a general exile in 586 B.C. at which time the temple and city were burned. All survivors, except except the poorest of the land, were taken to Babylon (II Kings 24:20-25:21; Jeremiah 39:1-10). It has been estimated, on the basis of all known data, that the captives to Babylon did not exceed 70,000 people.

In 538 B.C., Cyrus, the Persian king, overthrew the Babylonian empire. He subsequently issued a decree permitting the Hebrews to return to their land and to commence the rebuilding of their temple, which was begun in the spring of 536 B.C. (Cf.: Ezra 1:1-4; 6:3-5). The great leader of this return was Zerubbabel. A second return was accomplished in 457 B.C. under the scribe and reformer Ezra (Ezra 8). Finally, a third return was initiated under Nehemiah (Nehemiah 1-13). It has been estimated that the restored Jewish community numbered some 125,000 people (Cf.: Nehemiah 7:5-73). As a result of the captivity, the Hebrew people learned once and for all that Jehovah is the true God, and though they have been involved in many sins since that time, they were cured of idolatry!

The Inter-Biblical Period—With the completion of the Book of Malachi, the inspired literature of the Old Testament came to an end. Between the Old Testament and the beginning of the gospel era, there is a four hundred year period of history known as the "Inter-biblical Age." Since this is a "between-the-Testaments" period, we are dependent upon secular documents for a knowledge of the events of these centuries. Historical writings of this era include: (1) Greek and Roman writers (e.g., Xenophon, Herodotus); (2) Jewish documents (e.g., the Apocrypha, Josephus).

Politically, the age can be divided into three segments—Persian, Greek, and Roman.

During the **Persian** period, several significant things occurred. First, the political power of the Jewish High Priest greatly increased. Second, the synagogue system, which probably began during the Babylonian captivity, was more formally structered and used as a center of religious teaching. Third, the Aramaic language replaced Hebrew as the "spoken" tongue of the Jewish people (though Hebrew was retained for religious exercises).

The **Greek** era (332-167 B.C.) was also highly important for several reasons: (1) The Hebrews were greatly dispersed throughout Asia Minor, Egypt, Syria, etc., taking with them their Scriptures and the concept of one, true God. (2) In this age the Koine Greek language, the most accurately expressive language in human history, became the tongue of the entire civilized world. This was, of course, a providential preparation for the coming of the New Testament Scriptures. (3) The Septuagint (a Greek version of the Old Testament) was also produced during this time, thus making the prophecies concerning Jesus available to the Greek-speaking world.

The **Roman** period was also instrumental in preparing the way for the coming of Chirst in "the fulness of time" (Galatians 4:4). (1) An era of peace pervaded the civilized world; the *Pax Romana* (peace of Rome) brought East and West together, thus creating a climate in which the gospel could rapidly spread. (2) Roman engineering provided a magnificent system of highways which wonderfully accommodated that Great Commission, "Go ye into all the world...." (Mark 16:15). (3) The Roman legal system instilled a respect for law in the hearts of many, thus preparing the way for the "law of Christ" (Galatians 6:2).

In the inter-biblical age there also developed a number of the "sects" which are so prominent in New Testament history—the Pharisees, Sadducees, Herodians, Zealots, etc. The background of these groups is frequently important in understanding some of the events of the New Testament record.

The Life of Christ—The life of Jesus of Nazareth on the earth is the most important event in human history. According to the testimony of the prophets, Jesus was to be born in Bethlehem of Judea (Micah 5:2) to a virgin (Isaiah 7: 14). The New Testament reveals the precise fulfillment of those prophecies. Jesus was born around 4 B.C., according to our present calendar. The civil chronology, which is now used almost exclusively by the Western World, was introduced at Rome by Dionysius Exiguus in the sixth century A.D. It is generally agreed that the beginning of the Christian Era should have been fixed at least four years earlier.

Jesus Christ lived approximately thirty-three and one half years upon the earth, and most of the New Testament information deals with the final three and one half years of his life. The life of Christ may be divided into nine general periods. There are:

(1) **The Period of Preparation** (from his birth to his baptism—thirty years). (2) **A Period of Inauguration** (from his baptism to the rejection at Nazareth—fifteen months). (3) **The Early Galilean Ministry** (from the Nazareth rejection to the Sermon on the Mount—four months). (4) **The Later Galilean Ministry** (from the Sermon on the Mount to the feeding of the five thousand—ten months). (5) **A Period of Retirement** (from the feeding of the five thousand to the Feast of Tabernacles—six months). (6) **The Judean Ministry** (from the Feast of Tabernacles to the Feast of Dedication—three months). (7) **The Peraean Ministry** (from the Feast of Dedication to the anointing at Bethany—four months). (8) **The Passion Week** (from the anointing at Bethany to the Resurrection—eight days). (9) **Post-resurrection Appearances** (from the Resurrection to the Ascension—forty days).

All of the events of the Lord's earthly sojourn are recorded in the gospel records of Matthew, Mark, Luke, and John, and in the first eleven verses of Acts 1.

The Establishment and Expansion of Christianity—The church of Christ was established on the day of Pentecost, some fifty days after the death of Christ. The record of the founding of the church is contained in Acts 2.

The first century church spans approximately seventy years (from 30 A.D. to 100 A.D.) and may be viewed in the following historical segments: (1) **The Jerusalem Church** (from the founding of the church on Pentecost to the death of Stephen—five years). (2) **The Expanding Church** (from the death of Stephen to the council at Jerusalem—fifteen years). (3) **The Church Among the Gentiles** (from the council at Jerusalem to the death of Paul—eighteen years). (4) **The Closing Years** (from the death of Paul to the death of John—thirty-two years).

CONCLUSION

The foregoing eleven periods of Bible history are, of course, quite abbreviated. They do, however, give the student a beginning point in putting the Bible story together, and no one, unfamiliar with these ages, can have a good, working knowledge of the Holy Scriptures.

Questions on Chapter 4

1. List the eleven periods of Bible history.

2. What word best describes the first eleven chapters of Genesis?

3. Who was the first person in the Bible to be called a "Hebrew?"

4. What was the religious significance of the ten plagues?

5. List four events that happened while Israel was encamped at Sinai.

6. Describe Israel's strategy in conquering Canaan.

7. Name the three kings of the "United Kingdom" period.

8. List four ways in which the evil Jeroboam altered the divine system of worship.

9. How was the kingdom of Judah eventually punished for her transgressions?

10. Name the leaders involved in the three returns from Babylonian Captivity.

11. Discuss the contributions of the Greeks and the Romans to the coming of Christ.

12. The ministry of Christ lasted approximately how long?

13. When was the church of Christ founded? Where is that recorded?

Chapter 5

THE BOOKS OF THE BIBLE—AN OVERVIEW

After one has familiarized himself with the basic historical periods of the Bible, he will want to know how and where the respective books of Scripture fit into the divine narrative. The next step in our study, therefore, will be to learn the main theme of each of the sixty-six books of the Bible. This can easily be accomplished in two weeks, with very little time invested each day, if one will simply practice reciting—alone or perhaps to a study partner—what he has learned. Work on about five books each day. [Note the italicized sections. Flashcards (with the book name on the front and the summary on the back) might be helpful as a learning device.]

THE OLD TESTAMENT

Genesis—The first book of the Bible deals with **beginnings**. It reveals the beginning of: the universe, life, mankind, the home, sin, the plan of redemption, diverse languages, the Hebrew family, etc.

Exodus—The term "Exodus" means **departure** or **going out**. This book is the history of Israel's departure from Egyptian bondage and their consecration to God as a holy nation. It records the giving of the Law of Moses to the Hebrew nation.

Leviticus—The title denotes "that which pertains to the Levites," the **priestly** tribe. This book gives information regarding sacrifices, the priesthood, purifications, and festivals of the Mosaic system.

Numbers—This book is the record of Israel's **forty-year** sojourn in the **wilderness of Sinai**. It derives its name from the census figures prominent in the document.

Deuteronomy—The title means "second law." It is a **rehearsal of the Law of Moses** for the new generation that was about to enter the land of Canaan (the older generation having died in the wilderness).

Joshua—The book is the account of Israel's **conquest of Canaan** under the leadership of Joshua, thus demonstrating the fulfillment of the "land promise" to the patriarchs.

Judges—This narrative deals with the rule of **the fifteen Judges** (deliverers/leaders) during the period of the **settlement** of Canaan, when Israel went through alternating cycles of apostasy and repentance.

Ruth—This is the beautiful story of Ruth, a Moabite woman in the days of the Judges, who was providentially incorporated by God into the Hebrew family to be an **ancestress of David** (and thus of Christ).

I Samuel—This book contains the historical account of the **change in Israel's form of government** from the Judges to that of Kings. The nation desired a king to be like their pagan neighbors, thus rejecting the Lord as their sovereign Monarch. The record contains the history of Samuel and Saul.

II Samuel—This is the account of the **life and forty-year administration of David**, Israel's second king. It details his victories, sins, spiritual disposition, troubles, etc. David was the greatest of all Israel's kings.

I Kings—In this narrative is contained the record of the nation of Israel from the time of **David's death to the death of Jehoshaphat**, Judah's king. It covers the reign of Solomon, the division of the nation, and the conflicts between Elijah and Ahab, ruler of the northern kingdom Israel.

II Kings—II Kings is a history of the nation from the time of **Jehoshaphat's death until the period of Babylonian**

Captivity. The book records the closing days of Elijah, the ministry of Elisha, the Assyrian conquest of Israel, and the history of Judah between the Assyrian and Babylonian captivities.

I Chronicles—The purpose of this book is to re-acquaint the Jews of the post-Babylonian period with the history of David's reign. It stresses the priesthood and the temple during that era of Old Testament history.

II Chronicles—This document surveys the history of Judah and Jerusalem from the time of Solomon's reign through the Babylonian captivity for the post-captivity generation. It underscores the tragic departure of the Lord's people from his divine system.

Ezra—This book gives the history of Israel's first two returns from Babylonian Captivity. The first return was led by Zerubbabel in 536 B.C. and the second was under the leadership of Ezra in 457 B.C. It tells of the rebuilding of the temple that had been destroyed by the Babylonian invasion.

Nehemiah—The record of the final return from Babylonian Captivity under the leadership of Nehemiah. This occurred in 444 B.C. It tells the story of the rebuilding of Jerusalem's walls and the difficulties encountered in that endeavor.

Esther—This book contains the account of the marvelous providential preservation of the Jewish people by means of Queen Esther. The setting is in Persia between the time of the first and second returns from Babylonian Captivity.

Job—The book is an ancient drama depicting the suffering of Job, who demonstrated that God is worthy of trust and service, even when one's health and physical blessings are virtually gone. It shows that the righteous are not exempt from affliction and that patience is a great virtue.

Psalms—Psalms is a collection of 150 songs of praise by a variety of authors (37 attributed to David). They emphasize the authors' relationship with Jehovah. They stress the Lord's power in creation and his sovereignty over nature. The Psalms reveal an awareness of Israel's redemptive role in the coming of the Messiah.

Proverbs—The book of Proverbs is a **collection of wise sayings**, many written by Solomon, which instruct the reader in the application of divine wisdom to a variety of life experiences in an evil world. They span more than two centuries in composition.

Ecclesiastes—This great work demonstrates that earthly goals, pursued as ends, lead only to emptiness. Neither wealth, human wisdom, pleasure, etc. can bring happiness. The **duty of man** is to fear Jehovah and to keep his commandments.

Song of Solomon—This is one of the many songs written by King Solomon (he wrote 1,005). It extols the passion and **bliss of wedded love**. The song glorifies marriage and celebrates the virtues of the king's "beloved."

Isaiah—Isaiah is the Messianic prophet. He foretells **coming judgments** (upon Israel, Judah, and various nations) and yet, **future comfort** as well. Judgment is the punishment for sin, but there will be relief: first, from the period of captivity but then ultimately, a spiritual blessing in the advent of the Messiah.

Jeremiah—In a day of great spiritual corruption, Jeremiah **offers God's final invitation to rebellious Judah**. When Judah rejects his message, he foretells the Babylonian Captivity and urges the nation not to resist Jehovah's chastisement. He was greatly persecuted for his courageous message.

Lamentations—This composition was also by Jeremiah. It is a **funeral dirge written to commemorate the destruction of Jerusalem** as that city was utterly demolished by the Babylonians in 586 B.C. The song is also a sad reminder of Judah's sins which precipitated that horrible calamity.

Ezekiel—False prophets had declared to Judah that her captivity in Babylon would be only temporary (not the full seventy years). Ezekiel declares otherwise and **warns the nation against the false hope of an early return**. He also projects forward to the glories of the Christian age.

Daniel—Daniel, as a captive in Babylon, pens this great

book to declare **Jehovah's sovereign control over the nations**. National "goodness" is rewarded and "evil" is punished. As a token of hope, he depicts the coming kingdom of God which, unlike the political powers of this world, will stand for ever.

Hosea—Hosea lived just prior to the Assyrian captivity. His mission was to **admonish the northern kingdom for her idolatry** (Baal worship), and to urge her repentance. Hosea's own adulterous wife is used to illustrate Israel's sin and the Lord's continuing love for His beloved people.

Joel—Joel, a prophet of the southern kingdom, warns of the coming judgmental **day of the Lord** on account of Israel's sinful conduct. The punishment is described under the figure of a dreaded plague of locust. Blessings, however, will come to the faithful.

Amos—During a period of **ease and vice in the northern kingdom**, the prophet cries out against idolatry and immorality. He warns of judgment upon Israel and the nations, but speaks of a spiritual restoration in the work of Christ.

Obadiah—This book contains prophecies of the **impending doom of Edom** (the descendants of Esau, the brother of Jacob) on account of her sins—particularly her unkind treatment of her brethren, the Israelites. The nations will also be judged.

Jonah—This narrative is a record of **God's foreign missionary (Jonah) to the people of Nineveh**. In a time of Israel's apostasy and smug spirit of national exclusivism, Jehovah demonstrates his international interests.

Micah—This prophet cried out against **corruption and injustice in Judah** during the reigns of Jotham, Ahaz, and Hezekiah. He prophesied of coming punishment for wickedness.

Nahum—Under the preaching of Jonah, Nineveh, the capital of Assyria, had repented and Jehovah had spared those people. Later, though, they fell again into great wickedness. Nahum's mission is thus to declare **the full end of Nineveh**.

Habakkuk—This book raises a theological issue. How

can the Lord, consistent with his holiness, use a nation as evil as **Babylon to destroy Judah?** The answer is: when he has employed Babylon as the instrument of his wrath to chastize his people, he will punish that nation as well!

Zephaniah—Zephaniah's great preaching took place just **before King Josiah's reformation.** He spoke of the impending judgment upon Judah and her heathen neighbors. There is, though, hope in the Messianic age of several centuries later.

Haggai—After Judah's initial return from Babylon (536 B.C.), work had commenced on the temple, but then it was delayed due to opposition and discouragement. Haggai's mission is to **encourage the completion of the temple.**

Zechariah—As Haggai was admonishing Judah to rebuild the temple, his contemporary, Zechariah, was seeking to lead the nation into a climate of **spiritual rebuilding.** He urged the restoration of a close relationship to Jehovah.

Malachi—During the final years of the Old Testament era the Lord's people fell into a state of spiritual deadness. Malachi **attacks Judah's religious indifference** and calls for repentance. He heralds the coming of John the Baptizer.

THE NEW TESTAMENT

Matthew—This first New Testament book is designed to prove, on the basis of Old Testament evidence, that **Jesus of Nazareth is the promised Messiah.** It was thus an apologetic document (directed to the Jews) and a great source of comfort for the first century saints.

Mark—Mark's account is directed to the **Romans, stressing that Christ is that servant of God** who came to earth to accomplish Heaven's will. It emphasizes the deeds of Jesus and also gives careful attention to his emotions.

Luke—This narrative was designed for the **Greeks** and it calls attention to the **humanity** of the Lord. The document evidences a great interest in the Gentiles. It records eleven prayers of Christ.

John—John's record is a **universal gospel**. It was written to convince all men that Jesus is the Christ, the Son of the living God (20:30, 31). It gives emphasis to the "signs" performed by Christ, and focuses upon the "passion week."

Acts—The book is a record of the **establishment and expansion of the church** which Christ had promised to build (Matthew 16:18). It is a case-book on "conversion," ten examples of conversion to Christ being found therein.

Romans—This letter from Paul to the saints in Rome argues for **God's plan of justification, by means of faith, through the gospel system.** Justification before God is not through the law of Moses, but is on the basis of obedient faith in Jesus.

I Corinthians—The epistle is to Christians in the wicked city of Corinth. It deals with a multitude of **local church problems** and answers a variety of questions that had been submitted to the apostle Paul.

II Corinthians—Paul's second recorded letter to the church in Corinth. It urges forgiveness for an erring but penitent brother, encourages the completion of a promised benevolent contribution for Jewish Christians, and makes a **defense of Paul's apostleship** against certain critics.

Galatians—A Jewish element in the church taught that submission to the law of Moses, as well as obedience to Christ, was essential to pardon. This letter declares that Christians are not under the Mosaic system; we have **liberty in Christ**—though not license to sin.

Ephesians—The book sets forth a divine philosophy of world history by affirming that the **fulfillment of God's eternal purpose is accomplished in Christ.** It reveals the beauty and value of the church as the bride of Jesus Christ.

Philippians—This narrative is a **love letter from Paul to his favorite church**, the Philippian congregation. It expresses thanksgiving for their support, encourages unity among the brethren, and offers words of encouragement under persecution.

Colossians—The letter to the Colossians is Paul's refutation of a certain Judaeo-Gnostic heresy. Positively, it argues for the **supremacy of Christ** over the creation, human philosophy, angels, etc.

I Thessalonians—In this great letter, Paul commends the faith of these brethren, defends his apostleship against his critics, and, due to an apparent disturbance in the church, encourages Christian responsibility in view of the second **coming of Christ**.

II Thessalonians—This letter seeks to correct an erroneous idea advocated by some in Thessalonica, namely that the **day of the Lord is at hand**. The apostle calls for discipline upon idle speculators and warns of a great departure from the faith, which, in fact, was already beginning to work.

I Timothy—A letter of **instruction to a young evangelist**. Paul cautions Timothy against false prophets, teaches concerning worship, elders, deacons, and evangelists, and warns of those who would fall away from the faith and proclaim demonic doctrines.

II Timothy—This is Paul's final letter. It summons Timothy to Rome, where the apostle is imprisoned. It is designed to **help the young evangelist understand** the events that are occurring there. It contains the apostle's **farewell charge**.

Titus—Paul's letter to Titus directed to assist this preacher in **properly organizing the Christian work on the island of Crete**. It gives instructions to (and concerning) various groups (e.g., elders, men, women) in the church there.

Philemon—This is an **intercessory letter on behalf of a run-away slave**. In Rome, Paul had converted Onesimus, a slave who had left Philemon of Colossae. Paul sends the servant home, encouraging his owner to now receive him as a useful brother.

Hebrews—Judaizers were encouraging some first century saints to abandon Christianity and revert to the Mosaic system. Hebrews is written to show the **superiority of the New Cove-**

51

nant over the **Old Covenant**. It has a better: Prophet, Priesthood, Promises, Hope, etc.

James—This powerful little book is designed to encourage Christians during a time of persecution and to urge them to incorporate the principles of Christian responsibility into their lives daily. It has been called **the gospel of practical Christianity**.

I Peter—This is an epistle to **dispersed Christians who are enduring persecution**. It exhorts the brethren to faithfulness, testifies of the true grace of God, and admonishes brethren to suffer hardship for Christ.

II Peter—This letter is a caustic warning against false teachers who were advocating **destructive heresies** concerning the nature of Christ, sensual indulgence, the coming of Christ, the end of the world, etc.

I John—John's first epistle is a refutation of **gnostic errors** (an early sect claiming supernatural "knowledge"). It addresses the deity and humanity of Jesus and encourages greater love for God and the brotherhood.

II John—This little book contains a **commendation of a certain elect lady**, and gives strong warnings concerning false teachers. They are not to be extended religious fellowship.

III John—The brief epistle gives **praise** for brethren like Gaius, yet **condemnation** for a church dictator such as Diotrephes.

Jude—This terse document was occasioned by the appearance of false teachers who denied the Lord who brought them. It gives many Old Testament examples of apostasy and encourages the brethren to **contend for the faith**.

Revelation—The final book of the New Testament is a symbolic narrative of encouragement during a time of bloody persecution. It predicts the overthrow of all forces that oppose God and admonishes Christians to **overcome and the victory will be theirs**.

The foregoing is a summary of the main messages of each of the sixty-six books of the Bible. The student must now memorize a **key word or phrase** associated with each of these books that will bring to mind the basic theme of the document. The following chart is suggested for memory work.

OLD TESTAMENT BOOKS

Genesis . . . . beginnings
Exodus . . . . departure
Leviticus . . . . priesthood
Numbers . . . . wilderness wandering
Deuteronomy . . . . second law
Joshua. . . . . .conquest
Judges . . . . settlement
Ruth . . . . ancestress
I Samuel . . . . Saul
II Samuel. . . . . David
I Kings. . . . . Solomon to Jehoshaphat
II Kings . Jehoshaphat to Babylonian Captivity
I Chronicles. David
II Chronicles .Solomon—Babylonian Captivity
Ezra. . . . . .return
Nehemiah . . . . rebuild
Esther . . . . Providence
Job . . . . patience
Psalms. . . . . praise
Proverbs . . . . .wisdom
Ecclesiastes . . . . duty
Song of Solomon. . . . . .wedded
Isaiah. . . . . judgment/comfort
Jeremiah . . . . invitation
Lamentations . . . . funeral
Ezekiel .false hope
Daniel . . . . nations
Hosea . . . . unfaithful wife
Joel. . . . . day of the Lord
Amos. ease in Zion

Obadiah . . . . Edom
Jonah . . . . Nineveh
Micah . . . . Israel/Judah
Nahum . . . . Nineveh's doom
Habakkuk . . . . Babylon
Zephaniah . . . . .Josiah
Haggai . . . . temple
Zechariah . . . . reformation
Malachi . . . . indifference

NEW TESTAMENT BOOKS

Matthew . . . . king
Mark . . . . servant
Luke . . . . man
John . . . . .deity
Acts . . . . conversion
Romans . . . . justification
I Corinthians . . . . problems
II Corinthians . . . . apostleship
Galatians . . . . liberty
Ephesians . . . . purpose
Philippians . . . . .affection
Colossians . . . . supremacy
I Thessalonians . . . . second coming
II Thessalonians . . . . apostasy
I Timothy . . . . .elder/deacon
II Timothy . . . . farewell
Titus . . . . .church order
Philemon . . . . .slave
Hebrews . . . . new covenant
James . . . . practical
I Peter . . . . .persecution
II Peter . . . . .heresies
I John . . . . love

II John . . . . commendation
III John. . . . . Diotrephes
Jude . . . . contend
Revelation. . . . . overcome

Questions on Chapter 5

1. Which Old Testament book deals with priestly ordinances?

2. The book of _____ relates the story of an ancestress of Jesus.

3. The book of Numbers records the events of Israel's _____ year sojourn in the Wilderness of Sinai.

4. What is the difference between the books of II Samuel and I Chronicles?

5. Which Old Testament book is a "funeral song" over the destruction of Jerusalem?

6. What two words sum up the message of the book of Isaiah?

7. Who was the prophet that predicted the "full end" of Nineveh?

8. Which prophet prepared the way for king Josiah's reformation?

9. Discuss the respective thrusts of Matthew, Mark, Luke and John.

10. List the ten cases of conversion recorded in Acts.

11. What New Testament letter deals with a runaway slave?

12. In _____ Paul deals with local church problems and answers questions submitted by these brethren to him.

Chapter 6

ANALYZING THE BOOKS OF THE BIBLE

After one has savored the flavor of each of the sixty-six books of the Bible, that is, he has acquainted himself with the general thrust of each narrative, he will surely want to further explore the basic design of each document in greater detail. Who was the author of the book (if such is known)? When did he live and with what historical time-frame is he dealing? For whom, specifically, was the book designed (of course, ultimately, the whole of the Bible is for the benefit of man generally)? What are the main sections of each book? How has the author developed his theme? These are crucial questions that must engage the attention of the serious Bible student.

AUTHORSHIP

The important thing to remember about the Bible is that its ultimate Author is God Almighty! Every scripture is inspired of Him (II Timothy 3:16). Be that as it may, the Lord used human instruments through whom to bring his message to the world. In many instances we can know precisely who the human authors were that recorded the words of the sacred text; in other cases, we do not know who penned the documents. Obviously, it is not necessary that we know—otherwise Jehovah would have informed us!

In some situations it is important that one have a know-

56

ledge of who wrote a particular biblical book. For example, in Acts 18, on his second missionary campaign, the apostle Paul came to the city of Corinth. First, he proclaimed the gospel among the Jews in the synagogue. When they turned a deaf ear to his message, he commenced to evangelize among the Gentiles. Those who gladly received his message (whether Jew or Greek) were immersed and thus was the church of God at Corinth established (Acts 18:8). For the next year and a half, the apostle labored in that great Greek metropolis (Acts 18:11). Eventually, Paul resumed his journey, coming eastward to Ephesus. Here the tireless traveler remained for three years (cf. Acts. 20:31). While in Ephesus, Paul received word from Corinth (Cf.: I Corinthians 1:11) that the church there was troubled by internal dissension and doctrinal unsoundness. Accordingly, from Ephesus (Cf.: I Corinthians 16:8), the apostle Paul penned I Corinthians, the design of which was to address these church problems and to answer certain inquiries sent to him by those brothers in the Lord. It is thus important, from a historical perspective, to understand that Paul authored the epistle to the Lord's church in Corinth (Cf.: I Corinthians 1:1, 2).

On the other hand, the specific authorship of a particular biblical book frequently is not critical to the message of the narrative. Who wrote the books of I and II Samuel? No one really knows. Samuel himself might have written certain portions of the book [in the Hebrew text, I and II Samuel are one document] , but since many of the events in the account extend well beyond his life-time, some have speculated that portions were penned by perhaps Gad, Nathan, or Abiathar. Who wrote the book of Hebrews? Countless hours have been expended by speculators who have sought to determine the writer of this marvelous New Testament document, but it has all been for nought. In the final analysis, as Origin (one of the early "church fathers") expressed it, "Only God knows for certain." I have long appreciated the statement of Professor Stibbs in this connection: "When a human writer of Scripture was providentially led to hide his identity there is no need to try, and possibly little hope of success in trying, to discover it. It is wiser to be content not to know" (*The New Bible Commentary: Revised*, Eerdmans, 1970, p. 1191).

THE RECIPIENTS

It is sometimes very important to know who the recipients of a particular book were. For instance, one can really fully appreciate the synoptic gospel accounts [Matthew, Mark, and Luke] only if he understands that these narratives were directed to three different cultural elements of first century society. Matthew's account is directed to the **Jewish** mind, Mark's record has a decidedly **Roman** flavor, and Luke's narrative is designed to appeal to the **Greek** mode of thinking. Again, though, sometimes no particular recipients are suggested in the account. This is especially true for many of the historical narratives, poetical books, etc.

If possible, therefore, one should determine the author, the recipients, and the general circumstances that precipitated the writing of the various books of Scripture. The "Introduction" to the biblical books, as contained in some of the better conservative Bible commentaries, will frequently provide an invaluable service to the student in this regard.

ANALYZING THE CONTENT

Analyzing the content of the different books of the Bible is truly a thrilling chore; one that requires considerable effort, but pays rich rewards. There are two ways to approach the matter. Some books lend themselves to both **broad** analysis and **detailed** analysis. By this we mean that the book will, first of all, fall into a few very obvious major divisions; after the student has discovered these, he may then proceed to a more detailed study of each of these major sections. Let us first illustrate what we mean by these "larger" segments of the biblical documents.

Consider, for example, the book of Genesis. Moses, for the most part, divides this book into what one might term "genealogical" sections, each keyed by the word "generations." After a brief, historical introduction which sketches the creation of all things (Genesis 1:1—2:3), the author has ten divisions. They are:

1. The generations of the heavens and the earth (2:4—4:26).
2. The generations of Adam (5:1—6:8).
3. The generations of Noah (6:9—9:29).
4. The generations of Noah's sons (10:1—11:9).
5. The generations of Shem (11:10-26).
6. The generations of Terah (11:27—25:11).
7. The generations of Ishmael (25:12-18).
8. The generations of Isaac (25:19—35:29).
9. The generations of Esau (36:1-43).
10. The generations of Jacob (37:2—50:26).

Or consider the book of Exodus, it may be broadly divided in a couple of ways. It has three historical sections:

1. Egyptian bondage and deliverance (1—18).
2. The giving of the law of Moses (19—24).
3. The ordinances of the tabernacle and priesthood (25—40).

Or, the book may be given a two-fold division along spiritual lines:

1. Israel's redemption from bondage (1:1—15:21).
2. Israel's consecration to Jehovah (15:22—40:38).

Look at the book of I Kings. It contains two major sections, easily remembered:

1. The **United** Kingdom under Solomon (1—11).
2. The **Divided** Kingdom of Israel and Judah [the first 83 years or so] (12—22).

Note how easily the book of Ezra divides:

1. The 1st return from captivity led by Zerubbabel (1—6).
2. The 2nd return from captivity led by Ezra (7—10).

Notice, if you will, that some ancient (but unknown) person has arranged the book of Psalms into five major "Books" [Cf.: the beginning of chapter 1, "Book I."]. Though the content of these sections varies considerably, the five "Books" may be generalized as follows:

Book I . . . . mostly prayers of David (1—41).
Book II . .deliverance of the godly from suffering (42—72).
Book III . . . . Jehovah's dealings with Israel (73—89).
Book IV . . the difficulties of the Lord's people (90—106).
Book V . . . . . . the glories of the Word of God (107—150).

The magnificent book of Isaiah has two major divisions:

1. Judgment from God [upon the nations, Israel and Judah] (1—39).
2. Comfort from God [in deliverance from captivity and in the coming Messiah] (40—66).

Just as the Bible has sixty-six books (39 in the Old Testament and 27 in the New Testament), so, the book of Isaiah has sixty-six chapters (39 in the first segment and 27 in the latter one).

In the New Testament, certain books also fall into easily remembered broad topics.

The book of Acts can be rather simply divided into two portions:

1. The growth of Christianity among the Jews (1—12).
2. The growth of Christianity among the Gentiles(13—28).

Note this brief outline of one of the more difficult books of the New Testament, Romans:

1. Paul's introduction (1:1-17).
2. Man, the sinner, in need of justification (1:18—3:20).
3. The plan of justification through Christ (3:21—7:25).
4. The results of justification (8:1-39).
5. Israel's rejection of justification (9:1—11:36).
6. Practical instruction, exhortation, greetings (12:1—16:27).

Observe how Paul's letter to the Galatians falls clearly into three parts.

1. Personal—a defense of his apostleship (1—2).
2. Doctrinal—freedom from the law and liberty in Christ (3—4).
3. Practical—in your freedom, walk by the Spirit, not by the lusts of the flesh (5—6).

It is so rewarding to carefully work your way through the Bible, noting the broad, general sections of the sacred narratives. Let me recommend this program. Determine to broadly analyze five books of the Bible **per week** over the next three months or so. Make a notebook of these brief outlines; when you are satisfied with your short outline for a particular book, copy it into your study Bible at the beginning of that book. Henceforth, when you are ready to read in that narrative, you will have before you a brief reminder of what the material is all about. Later, we will mention several books which will be helpful in this exercise.

DETAILED ANALYSIS

The books of Scripture, being ultimately from God Himself and conveyed through the hands of inspired men, were obviously given according to an intelligent plan. It is the solemn task of the dedicated Bible student, therefore, in approaching the various biblical documents, to discover how the author has arranged or developed his material. In order to accomplish such a task, a somewhat detailed analysis of the general contents of the account is required. But the novice student may find himself quite frustrated at this point, not knowing just where or how to commence such a project.

First of all, as we suggested in the previous portion of this chapter, one should attempt to discover the major sections of the narrative. There are several inexpensive books that are quite helpful in this connection. In his little volume, *The Bible Book By Book*, (Moody, 1955), G. Coleman Luck has brief outlines on each book of the Bible. Similarly, William Deal in his work, *Baker's Pictorical Introduction to the Bible* (Baker, 1967) has concise outlines that will assist one in getting oriented as to the major divisions of the book that he is studying. [NOTE: One must be cautious, for some of these authors include erroneous "millennial" dogma even in their outlines.] Observe, for example, Deal's outline of the book of Joshua.

I. Introduction and qualifying of Joshua (1:1-18).
II. The conquest of Canaan (2—12).
III. The division of the land and the settling of Israel (13—22).
IV. Joshua's farewell address and last instructions (23—24).

With a general outline of the book in view, one can then proceed, as it were, to put "some meat on the bones." There are several devices that are helpful in accomplishing this. The American Standard Version (1901) is arranged in paragraph form thus suggesting subtle changes in subject matter. Some of the modern "study Bibles" have divided the biblical chapters into sections and given them sub-titles, which frequently is quite helpful.

To do a detailed outline (analysis) of a biblical book is not an easy task, and some folks, simply because they do not like to **think** and **work**, avoid such projects. In so doing, though, they rob themselves of a valuable approach to the subject matter.

Let us take a couple of biblical books, as examples, of this method of study, and attempt an outline analysis.

Earlier we mentioned that the book of Isaiah conveniently falls into two major sections: Judgment from God (1—39); Comfort from God (40—66). Let us develop these points.

THE BOOK OF ISAIAH

I. Judgment from God (1—39).
  A. Prophecies concerning Judah and Jerusalem (1—12).
    1. Isaiah and his time (1:1)
    2. Judah's rebellion and coming punishment (1:2-31).
    3. The glorious Messianic Age (2:1-4).
    4. Judah's present wickedness (2:5-11).
    5. A day of reckoning to come (2:12-22).
    6. Judah's punishment and glory (3:1—4:6).
    7. Judah's sins (5:1-30).
    8. Isaiah's vision and commission (6:1-13).
    9. War against Jerusalem (7:1-9).
    10. The Lord's "sign"—Messiah (7:10-16).
    11. Judah's coming desolation (7:17-25).
    12. The Assyrian invasion (8:1—10:34).
    13. Judah's hope in the coming Christ (11:1—12:6).
  B. Prophecies concerning foreign nations (13—23).
    1. Babylon (13:1—14:27).
    2. Philistia (14:28-32).

3. Moab (15:1—16:14).

4. Damascus—and Israel (17:1-14).

5. Ethiopia (18:1-7).

6. Egypt (19:1—20:6).

7. Babylon (21:1-10).

8. Edom and Arabia (21:11-17).

9. An oracle concerning Jerusalem (22:1-25).

10. Tyre and Sidon (23:1-18).

C. Judgments upon the nations (24—27).

1. Judgment—the consequence of sin (24:1-23).

2. Jehovah will deliver Zion (25:1-12).

3. Judah's consolation (26:1-21).

4. Oppressors punished/faithful delivered (27:1-13).

D. A book of woes (28—35).

1. Woe to Israel (28:1-13).

2. Woe to Judah (28:14-22).

3. Woe to Ariel [Jerusalem] (29:1-24).

4. Woe to those who seek Egypt's aid (30:1—31:9).

5. Salvation to come (32:1—33:24).

6. Wrath upon the nations/Zion's glorious future (34:1—35:10).

E. A historical section (36—39).

1. The Assyrian invasion (36:1—37:38).

2. Hezekiah's deliverance (38:1-22).

3. Babylonian captivity foretold (39:1-8).

II. Comfort from God (40—66).

A. Deliverance from Babylonian Captivity (40—48).

1. The greatness of God (40:1-31).

2. The Lord's challenge to heathenism (41:1-29).

3. Promises concerning Jehovah's servant (42:1-25).

4. Judah's projected redemption from captivity (43:1-28).

5. The futility of idolatry (44:1-23).

6. God's use of Cyrus—the deliverer (44:24—45:13).

7. The Lord's power over the nations (45:14-25).

8. Babylon's idols versus the true God (46:1-13).
9. The impending fall of Babylon (47:1-15).
10. Deliverance from captivity (48:1-22).
B. Jehovah's suffering servant (49—57).
  1. Scope of the servant's ministry (49:1-6).
  2. The joyful return (49:7-13).
  3. The spiritual restoration of Zion (49:14-26).
  4. Jehovah's faithful servant (50:1-11).
  5. Israel exhorted to trust God (51:1-23).
  6. Israel admonished to return to the Lord (52:1-12).
  7. The servant's suffering and victory (52:13—53:12).
  8. The blessings of the new Zion (54:1-17).
  9. Extension of Jehovah's mercy (55:1-13).
  10. Universal blessings to the obedient (56:1-18).
  11. A rebuke of corrupt leaders (56:9—57:21).
C. The glory of the Messianic age (58—66).
  1. A contrast between false and true worship (58:1-14).
  2. The effect of sin (59:1-8).
  3. A confession of national wickedness (59:9-21).
  4. The glory of the redeemed (60:1-22).
  5. The "Jubilee" of God's favor (61:1-11).
  6. The glory of spiritual Zion (62:1-12).
  7. Punishment of the nations (63:1-6).
  8. Lessons from history (63:7-14).
  9. A prayer for victory (63:15—64:12).
  10. The destiny of the righteous and the wicked (65:1-25).
  11. A final rebuke (66:1-9).
  12. Spiritual Zion's glorious future (66:10-24).

An outline, such as the foregoing, would be essential if one intended to effectively teach the book of Isaiah.

Let us now briefly look at one of the New Testament books. On his second missionary journey, Paul entered the city of Philippi (Acts 16:12). With the conversion of Lydia and her household, the first church of Christ was established on European soil. A close bond developed between the apostle and this church and some ten years later, he writes to them in his "Epistle to the Philippians." Here is how one might approach a study of this tender "love letter" from an apostle to his favorite church.

THE EPISTLE OF PAUL TO THE PHILIPPIANS

1. The salutation (1:1,2).
   A. From Paul, along with his companion Timothy.
   B. Addressed to the bishops, deacons, and saints in the city of Philippi.

II. Paul's thanksgiving and prayer for the Philippian brethren (1:3-11).
   A. Paul is thankful for their fellowship in the gospel from the first day until the present time (1:3-5).
   B. He expresses confidence that God's work in them will be completed (1:6-8).
   C. The apostle prays for their spiritual growth (1:9-11).

III. Paul's personal circumstances (1:12-26).
   A. The progress of the gospel in Rome is discussed (1:12-14).
   B. Paul has rivals in Rome who are attempting to make things difficult for him; their motives are wrong (1:15-18).
   C. Whatever the circumstances, the apostle hopes that Christ will be magnified (1:19-26).

IV. Exhortations from Paul (1:27—2:18).
   A. Paul appeals for the brethren to be united (1:27—

2:4).

    B. Humility is the key to unity and Christ is the great example of that (2:5-11).

    C. The apostle gives practical admonitions which encourage obedience (2:12-18).

V.   The apostle's immediate plans (2:19-30).

    A. He intends to send his companion Timothy to assist them as soon as possible (2:19-24).

    B. Epaphroditus, their minister to Paul, will be returned to them presently (2:25-30).

VI.   Paul warns about false teachers (3:1—4:1).

    A. Beware of Judaizing teachers (3:1-3).

    B. Paul gives credibility to his warning by discussing his own Hebrew background (3:4-6).

    C. The apostle lists the things which he had gladly forfeited for the cause of Christ (3:7-9).

    D. He affirms his burning desire to obtain the great goal (3:10-16).

    E. Paul gives a caustic warning concerning these enemies of the cross of Christ (3:17—4:1).

VII.   Some concluding words of encouragement (4:2-9).

    A. Paul attempts to heal a breech between two feuding Christian women (4:2,3).

    B. There is great joy in being in Christ (4:4-7).

    C. Thinking on the right things will produce sound mental health (4:8,9).

VIII.   Paul's acknowledgment of Philippi's support of his work (4:10-20).

    A. The apostle has learned to be content in any condition (4:10-13).

    B. There is much reward in the generous support of the gospel (4:14-20).

IX. The closing (4:21-23).
    A. Salutations are extended to, and from, brethren in the Lord (4:21,22).
    B. Paul prays that the grace of Christ will abide with his beloved brethren (4:23).

With these examples before you, you are encouraged to begin your personal "detailed analysis" of some of the books of the Bible. Be patient and persistent; it will get easier!

Questions on Chapter 6

1. It is sometimes important to know the author of a biblical book; sometimes it is not. Can you give examples of each?

2. Name the respective recipients of Matthew, Mark, and Luke.

3. What is the key word that separates the divisions of the book of Genesis?

4. What are the two major divisions of I Kings?

5. Give a three-fold outline of Galatians.

6. List the two major sections of the book of Isaiah.

7. Name the first church of Christ on European soil.

8. What two words would stress a two-fold **spiritual** division of the book of Exodus.

9. The book of Psalms has been divided into _____ major "Books," containing a total of _____ psalms.

10. Paul wrote to the Philippians approximately _____ years after he established that congregation.

Chapter 7

ANALYZING THE BIBLE BY CHAPTERS

It is probably safe to say that more people do their Bible studying (reading) by chapters than in any other way. This is not the most effective way to study the Scriptures, but if one wishes to approach the text in this manner, he can learn a great deal of the Bible. In this section of our work, we will devote attention to the selection and analysis of some of the great chapters in the Holy Scriptures.

The ancient Jews divided the Pentateuch into fifty-four *parshioth* (sections), one of which was read in the synagogue each Sabbath (Cf.: Acts 13:15). These sections were later subdivided into 669 *sidrim* or orders. The New Testament was also divided into certain portions at an early period in its history. Our **modern** division of the text into chapters is generally attributed to cardinal Hugo of St. Cher in about 1240 A.D., who also produced a Concordance for the Latin Vulgate. It might be noted, however, that a cardinal Humbert, about 1559, cited Exodus 12, 13, and Leviticus 23, **according to our present division of chapters**.

There are 1,189 chapters in the entire Bible. If the student examined one chapter per day, it would take him about three years and three months to work his way through the entire sacred volume.

Some chapters of the Bible will obviously be more pertinent and practical than others. We believe, however, that there are precious nuggets of truth in **every** chapter for those who

69

have the skill and patience to dig them out. Almost all of the biblical chapters, either partially or wholly, have within them a definite development, and it is ascertaining this development that yields the richest treasures. Let us select some examples to illustrate this wonderful method of investigation.

It is certainly not surprising that one of the most important chapters in the Bible is the very first one. Moses, the author of Genesis, has elsewhere informed us that the **entire** creation (the heaven and earth, the sea, and all that is in them) was made in six days (**literal** days—the same type as the Sabbath—Exodus 20:8-11). Genesis one forms a marvelous six-point outline of those events.

THE CREATION ACTIVITY OF GOD
Genesis One

I. Day One (1—5)
   A. The creation by God in the beginning (1)
   B. The earth initially formless and empty (2a)
   C. The organizing activity of the Spirit (2b)
   D. Creation of light and its separation from darkness (3,4)
   E. The naming of earth's light and darkness (5)

II. Day Two (6—8)
   A. The creation of an "expanse" between the waters above and the waters below (6,7)
   B. The expanse is named "heaven" (8)

III. Day Three (9—13)
   A. Earth's waters gathered together into one place and dry land appears (9)
   B. Land and waters named (10)
   C. Earth puts forth grass, herbs yielding seed, and fruit trees, each after its kind (11—13)

IV. Day Four (14—19)
   A. Heavenly luminaries created and their purpose stated (14,15)
   B. Sun, moon, and stars (16—19)

V. Day Five (20—23)
   A. Sea creatures and birds are made, after their kind (20—23)

VI. Day Six (24—31)
   A. Earth's creatures—wild and domestic—made (24,25)
   B. Man and woman created (26,27)
   C. Mankind commissioned to fill the earth and subdue it (28)
   D. Food supply for earth's creatures (29,30)
   E. God's evaluation of His creation—very good (31)

With careful research, the foregoing outline could be greatly expanded and thus form the basis of a series of classes, sermons, etc.

One of the most popular chapters of the entire Bible is Psalm 23. It has been called the "Nightingale Psalm," for as the nightingale sings so sweetly at the midnight hour, so this psalm has calmed many a midnight hour in the lives of men. The 23rd Psalm may be analyzed in the following way.

First, there is a general proposition affirmed: Jehovah is a good Shepherd who cares for His people; they are amply supplied in Him (vs. 1). The proposition is then demonstrated by two lines of argument: (1) Jehovah is a provider (vss. 2-4); Jehovah is a protector (vs. 5). Finally, there is a confident affirmation that results from these premises (vs. 6). Let us look more closely at this masterpiece in outline form.

I. The Proposition: The author of the Psalm (David, according to the superscription) expresses his confidence in Jehovah. The Lord will care for him as a shepherd tenderly looks after his sheep. He will, therefore, not be in want in any essential way for his spiritual well-being (1).

II. The Proposition Proved (2—6).
   A. Jehovah sustains our constant needs (2—4).
      1. He makes us to lie down (in the hot mid-day heat—cf.: Song of Solomon 1:7) in green pastures (where there is abundant nourishment).
      2. He leads (gently guides—the shepherd does not "drive" the sheep) us by still waters (waters of rest and refreshment—cf.: Isaiah 32:18).
      3. He restores our souls, i.e., He renews and sustains our spiritual lives.
      4. He leads (guides) us in paths of righteousness (right conduct) for His name's sake (demonstrating His personal integrity—cf.: Exodus 34:5ff).
      5. Though we walk through the valley of the shadow of death (perilous places), we fear no (ultimate) evil, for God is with us; His presence is His people's strength and comfort (Cf.: Genesis 28:15; Joshua 1:5ff).
      6. The Lord's rod and staff (the shepherd's crook by which he rescues the sheep from dangerous places and wards off the enemy—cf.: II Samuel 23:21; Psalm 2:9; Micah 7:14) give a sense of security (comfort).
   B. Jehovah, as a gracious host, protects us (5,6).
      1. As a "host," the Lord shows us special favor by preparing for us a bountiful table of good things.
      2. We can enjoy such a treat even though our enemies are near, for we trust in God's care to do for

us what is best.

3. Jehovah annoints our heads with oil (a sweet token of His favor—cf.: Psalm 45:7; 92:10; Amos 6:6).

4. Our cup overflows (the Lord is not stingy with His blessings—cf.: Luke 6:38).

III. The confident conclusion (6).
A. The Lord's is with us always.
1. Unlike the wicked, who are pursued by warnings of God's judgment and vengeance (Cf.: Romans 12:19; 14:10), goodness and mercy follow the saint throughout life.
B. The firm resolution (6).
1. Because of the Lord's graciousness, the faithful will thus make his abode in God's house (i.e., in His spiritual presence—cf.: Psalm 36:8) for the remainder of his days.

This wonderful masterpiece of biblical literature is absolutely filled with instruction and comfort!

One of the most thrilling chapters of divine truth in the Old Testament is surely Isaiah 53. It is a veritable galaxy of prophecies concerning that "Lamb of God" who beareth away the sin of the world (Cf.: John 1:29). It has long been customary for many Jews and liberal Bible critics to allege that Jehovah's "suffering servant" of this chapter alludes to the distresses of the **Jewish nation** at the hand of the Romans in 70 A.D., and not to Jesus of Nazareth. This theory, however, is clearly at variance with the evidence as the following contrasts will reveal:

(1) The suffering one is a "he," "him," contrasted with the "we" and "our," which allude to the nation.

(2) The suffering servant voluntarily gave Himself; the Jewish nation never did.

(3) The suffering servant was an innocent victim, the Jewish nation was guilty of many sins.

(4) The suffering of the servant secured pardon for others, such was never the case with the Jewish nation.

(5) The suffering servant did not resist His death, the Jewish nation vigorously resisted the Romans.

(6) The writers of the New Testament declare that Christ is the Lamb that was slain, not the Hebrew nation.

In view of these considerations, let us look analytically at this beautiful chapter.

ISAIAH 53—CHRIST, THE ATONING LAMB

I. The Jews' disbelief in Jesus as the Messiah is foretold (1).
   A. The two questions: "Who has believed our report? and to whom has Jehovah's arm been revealed?", suggest the Jewish rejection of Heaven's message concerning Christ, and a disbelief in the miracles which the Lord performed (Cf.: John 12:37,38).
   B. It is thus clear that a rejection of Jesus Christ was equal to a rejection of God Himself (Cf.: Luke 10:16).

II. A description of Christ's rejection and suffering is given by the prophet (2,3).
   A. Jesus grew up as a tender plant and root out of dry ground—an indication of His humble beginnings and the unlikeliness of His success (from the human vantage point) (2a).
   B. His power was not to be in physical attraction (2b).
   C. Man's attitude toward the Messiah—despised and rejected (3a).
   D. His life was one of sorrow and grief (3b).
   E. He was unrecognized by most of His nation (3c).

74

III. The death of Christ was an atoning sacrifice on behalf of mankind (4—6).
   A. The substitutionary nature of the death of Christ is abundantly affirmed—He bore our griefs and sorrows, He received the stroke of God for our transgressions, He was wounded for us, our peace is secured by His suffering (4,5).
   B. The universal sinfulness of humanity is declared. All, like sheep, have gone astray(note: not "born astray"), but the way back is provided in Christ—Jehovah has laid on Him the iniquity of **all** (note: the atonement is theoretically **universal**, not, as Calvinism asserts, "limited" (6).

IV. The submissive disposition of Jesus during His trial and death is described (7).
   A. Though oppressed and afflicted, He made no verbal complaint (7a).
   B. Meekly, as a lamb that is led to the slaughter, He endured the cross (Cf.: John 1:29; Hebrews 12:2) (7b).

V. The legal proceedings in His death acknowledged His innocence (8).
   A. The official legal sentence in the case of Christ was "innocent" (Cf.: John 18:38; 19:4,6), yet, in spite of that, His judgment of innocence was "taken away" (Cf.: LXX; Acts 8:33) and He was treated as guilty (8a).
   B. The effect of His death would be so profound [His "generation" as seen in the church] that no one could adequately declare it (8b).
   C. Actually, however, His death was a part of the divine plan—for the transgression of the Lord's people (8c).

VI. The events of Christ's death were highly unusual (9).
   A. He was crucified as a felon (with thieves—Matthew

27:38), and, according to normal custom, He would have been disposed of as a wicked man (9a).

B. Amazingly, however, He was with the rich "in death," i.e., buried. He was interred in Joseph's tomb (Matthew 27:57-60). Man proposes; God disposes! (9b).

C. Yes, Christ was treated as a criminal even though He had perpetrated no violence, nor had He spoken deceit (9c).

VII. The death of Christ was the key element in the plan of God (10—12).

A. It was pleasing to God that His Son, through death, should become an "offering for sin" in order that man might be saved (10a).

B. His "days" were prolonged, however, in the resurrection from the dead, and He saw "his seed" (Cf.: Romans 7:4) in the establishment of His family (Cf.: I Timothy 3:15), the church (10b).

C. Through the Lord's work of bearing the sins of many, the justice of God is satisfied (11).

D. The cause of Christ is victorious—as one who takes the spoils in battle (12a).

E. He poured out his soul [life = blood—Leviticus 17:11] unto death—His life for ours! (12b).

F. Though Christ was treated as a transgressor in death, His entire ministry was an act of intercession for transgressors. Note His prayer in Luke 23:34.

What a tremendous difference it makes, in considering a chapter like Isaiah 53, when one studies it from an analytical viewpoint.

As one attempts to segment the chapters of the Bible according to the development of the various themes found therein, he should ask: what important lessons am I learning in these exercises? Let us pursue this matter in an examination of the first chapter of the New Testament.

Matthew, chapter 1, very naturally falls into four divisions as follows:

I.   The Genealogy of Jesus Christ (1–17).

II. The Miraculous Conception of Jesus Through the Power of the Holy Spirit (18,19).

III. The Angel's Announcement Concerning the Birth of Jesus (20,21).

IV. The Birth of Christ as Fulfillment of Prophecy (22–25).

Now, in this instance, instead of outlining the material according to the flow of the text, let us take each of these sections and note some of the great truths to be found.

I.   The Genealogy of Jesus Christ (1–17).
   1. Note the relationship between Christ and David and Abraham. The obvious suggestion is the connection of Christ to the prophecies made to these men (Genesis 22:18; II Samuel 7:12,13).
   2. Observe the tracing of the genealogy as a proof for the establishment of the Lord's qualification to the throne of David. Since all genealogical records of the Jews were destroyed by the Romans in the invasion of 70 A.D., the true Jewish Messiah must have already arrived prior to that time!
   3. Notice that, contrary to normal procedure, four women are mentioned in the genealogical record of Jesus—hinting of the elevated status that women would receive in the New Testament era (Cf.: Galatians 3:28).
   4. Some of those in this list are quite prominent for the tragic sins of their lives—Judah and Tamar, Rahab, David and Bathsheba, Solomon, etc., thus suggesting that Christ, though personally sinless (Hebrews 4:15), nevertheless had a lineal connection with sinners.

5. It is noteworthy that there were several Gentiles in the Lord's royal ancestry, e.g. Ruth, Rahab, perhaps foreshadowing the fact that Jesus was to be an international Savior (Mark 16:16).

6. Observe the incidental reference to Uriah's loss of his wife to David (6); inspiration preserves the moral blemishes even in the heroes of the Bible—an indication of the divine origin of the Book!

II. The Miraculous Conception of Jesus Through the Power of the Holy Spirit (18,19).
1. Mary did not illegitimately conceive, as the unbelieving Jews later argued. Rather, the conception was a miracle by the power of the Holy Spirit.

2. The compassionate character of Joseph, the man chosen by God to be the adoptive father of Jesus, is stressed.

III. The Angel's Announcement Concerning the Birth of Jesus (20,21).
1. God has used angels in the implemention of His plan
2. The mission of Jesus was to save His people from their sins. Something is thus revealed about the horrible nature of sin!

IV. The Birth of Jesus in Fulfillment of Prophecy (22—25).
1. One of the great evidences of Bible inspiration is that of predictive prophecy (Cf.: Isaiah 41:21ff). Seven centuries earlier, Isaiah had declared that "the virgin" [a particular woman] would conceive, bear a son [the sex specified] and His name would be called "Immanuel" [**God is with us**—suggesting the divine nature of the child] .

2. Joseph, a rational man, was convinced by the evidence to which he was exposed.

3. Joseph refrained from sexual intimacy with Mary un-

til after she gave birth to the Lord. The Roman Catholic dogma of the "perpetual virginity" of Mary is false (Cf.: Matthew 12:46).

LET'S SEE WHAT YOU HAVE LEARNED

In the earlier part of this chapter, I've been doing all the work. Now, it's time to let you, the student, put some of these ideas to work for yourself. The first example I'd like for you to "cut your teeth" on is the Savior's tender prayer, shortly before His arrest, as recorded in John 17. It is largely an intercessory prayer. The prayer easily falls into three sections. I will give you the subdivision titles and you will analyze the contents and supply the verses for each of these three sections.

Christ's Intercessory Prayer—John 17

I. The Lord prays for Himself (   ).

II. The Lord prays for His band of disciples (   ).

III. The Lord prays for all future believers (   ). [1]

Now that you've come through that with flying colors, let's try another exercise of a different type. One of the Master's greatest sermons was the "Sermon on the Mount." It consists of three chapters, 5—7, in the Gospel of Matthew. Let's analyze those chapters collectively. I will supply you with verse divisions this time, and you will fill in a phrase which summarizes this section. Later, you can compare you characterizations with mine.[2] Our phraseology may differ, of course, but we'll probably be close in thought. Here we go.

The Sermon on the Mount—Matthew 5-7

I.   (5:1-12)

II.   (5:13-16)

III.   (5:17-20)

IV.   (5:21-48)

V.   (6:1-18)

VI.   (6:19-24)

VII.   (6:25-34)

VIII.   (7:1-6)

IX.   (7:7-11)

X.   (7:12-14)

XI.   (7:15-20)

XII.   (7:21-27)

Let's try one more exercise before we conclude this chapter. In I Corinthians, chapters 12—14, Paul discusses certain problems associated with the "spiritual gifts" which had been bestowed upon certain of the Corinthian Christians. One of those problems had to do with the fact that some of those saints were exercising their gifts without proper consideration for their brethren. For example, one might employ his gift of a "tongue" [the ability to miraculously speak a foreign language] while someone else was speaking (thus creating confusion), or perhaps he would speak in the presence of those who did not understand the particular language characteristic of his gift (in such cases an interpreter would be needed). It was therefore needful that the apostle address this matter. In chapter 13 he does this in a two-fold way: first, he shows that those who are truly spiritual will use their gift in the context of a loving consideration for others, and not as an end within itself. Second, he argues that love is abiding, while the gifts are temporary. I Corinthians 13 falls into three parts. I will list these for you. In the spaces provided, you are to list some of the points and/or lessons learned from these sections.

I Corinthians 13

I. The Value of Love (1-3).

    A. _____

    B. _____

    C. _____

    D. _____

II. Love Defined (4—7).

    A. _____

    B. _____

    C. _____

    D. _____

III. The Abiding Nature of Love in Contrast to Temporary Spiritual Gifts (8—13).

    A. _____

    B. _____

    C. _____

    D. _____

CONCLUSION

If you learn to do more than simply "read" the chapters of the Bible, you will quickly learn that there are valuable truths to be discovered that have previously escaped your attention. Resolve to be a more scholarly Bible student!

---

[1] (1—5)
(6—19)
(20—26)

[2] 1. The Road to Blessedness (Happiness)
2. The Power of Influence
3. Jesus and the Law of Moses
4. The Responsibility of Christ's New System
5. The Futility of Superficial Service
6. True Treasure
7. The Vanity of Worry
8. The Wrong Kind of Judging
9. Persevering in Prayer
10. The Golden Rule and the Two Ways
11. Beware of False Teachers
12. The Two Builders

Chapter 8

TOOLS FOR BIBLE STUDY

Dr. T.W. Brents, a physician and outstanding preacher of the past century, once made a rather shocking statement. He said, "If you will show us a man who reads nothing but the Bible, we will show you one who reads and understands very little of that." Brents was not suggesting that the Bible is an insufficient guide to heaven; he was not contending that the Scriptures are unclear in essential matters relating to salvation. He was simply observing that it is the epitome of folly to ignore the labors of countless Bible scholars across the centuries who have made available, by means of the printed page, the results of their research. One of the wonders of the human mind is that it can build upon the knowledge of previous generations, and this is no less true of sacred knowledge.

Every Christian needs to build a personal religious library of good tools that will enhance his understanding of the Scriptures and his ability to convey that information to others. I have never known a well-informed, effective minister who did not have a good biblically related library. I have never met a truly knowledgable elder or Bible class teacher who did not at least have a few good books as study aids. In this chapter, we want to guide the average Christian in the selection of some basic biblical works which can help better qualify him for the noble task of teaching the Word of God. Keep in mind that this discussion is not designed for the specialist (ministers, Bible professors, etc.) who would require more extensive and technical tools in their work. We are merely addressing the average, humble Christian who just wants to be a better instructor.

A RELIABLE STUDY BIBLE

The first order of business is the obtaining of a reliable study Bible for your work in the text of the Scriptures. The most accurate, word-for-word translation currently available in the English language is the American Standard Version (1901 edition). Of course the King James Version is a reputable translation and it is still the favorite of many; it is, however, more than 350 years old, and the style is difficult for many to easily understand today. Recently, it has been revealed in a far more readable form, The New King James Version (Thomas Nelson Publishers, 1982), and it is a very fine study text.

Some of the more modern translations, such as the Revised Standard Version and the New International Version, have been criticized (and not without justification) due to the fact that there is considerable (erroneous) doctrinal bias incorporated into the biblical text. [For those who wish to study this matter in greater detail, we have addressed it in our booklet, *The Bible Translation Controversy* (Apologetics Press, Inc., 1985).] Be that as it may, however, these translations can be quite valuable as comparative aids, particularly in the study of the Old Testament. They frequently make the text much easier for the common person to understand.

CHRISTIAN EVIDENCES

Every Christian's library should contain a few books on Christian evidences. By this we mean works which address such critical issues as: the existence of God, the origin of man, the inspiration of the Bible, the deity of Christ, etc. We are living in a world of increasing naturalism, materialism, atheism, etc., and many people (unlike former generations) have no regard for the Bible at all. It is imperative, therefore, that the effective teacher arm himself/herself with some good material that will establish faith in God and the need to seek the counsel of his inspired Word. We will not take the space here to recommend volumes in this area of study; rather, we encourage the reader to write for a free catalog listing materials on Christian evidences available from: Apologetics Press, Inc., 230 Landmark Dr., Montgomery, Alabama 36117-2752.

BIBLE GEOGRAPHY

No serious student of the Scriptures can afford to be ignorant of the basic geography of the countries mentioned in the Bible. Where is the land of Canaan with reference to Ur of Chaldea (Abraham's original home)? Where are Egypt and the Wilderness of Sinai located relative to the Promised Land? Where was Caesarea-Philippi with reference to Jerusalem? Where were Paul's missionary campaigns carried out? These and a thousand other questions are vital to a proper understanding of numerous biblical situations. One's library should, therefore, contain at least one Bible atlas. We are recommending a few of the better ones.

Baker's Bible Atlas, Charles Pfeiffer (Baker Book House). Historical and archaeological information. 26 color maps. Charts, etc. 333 pages.

Zondervan Pictorical Bible Atlas, E.M. Blaiklock (Ed), (Zondervan Publishing Co.). Follows the chronology of the Bible events. 220 photos. 85 maps. 538 pages.

Wycliffe Historical Geography of Bible Lands, Charles Pfeiffer and Howard Vos (Eds). (Moody

Publishing Co.). Examines the biblical, historical, archaeological evidence relating to the Bible lands. 450 illustrations. 600 pages.

PRINCIPLES OF BIBLE INTERPRETATION

In chapter 3 of this work, we discussed some of the principles of Bible interpretation with which the student should become acquainted if he is to determine the meaning of the sacred text. The science of the Bible interpretation is technically called "hermeneutics," a term derived from the Greek *Hermes*, who, in Greek mythology, was alleged to be the "interpreter" of Jupiter. There are several good works available on hermeneutics.

Hermeneutics, D.R. Dungan (Standard). A textbook on the science of interpreting the Bible. 400 pages.

Interpreting The Bible, A. Berkeley Mickelson (Eerdmans). A comprehensive textbook on hermeneutics. Covers issues, methods, and tools.

Principles of Interpretation, Clinton Lockhart (Gospel Light). An excellent volume by a man of the restoration persuasion. Highly recommended for the average Christian. 260 pages.

Biblical Hermeneutics, Milton Terry (Zondervan). A classic work for the more advanced scholar. History and principles of interpretation. 782 pages.

BIBLE HISTORY

As we noted in an early chapter, if one is to appreciate the Bible in its proper historical perspective, he must have a feeling of the flow of biblical history. He should be familiar with the sequential development of the great events of Bible history. In order to facilitate this comprehension, the student should have at least one or two good volumes on Bible history. He should also be sure that such works are written from the conservative viewpoint. The following are several fine examples.

A History of Israel: From Conquest to Exile, John J. Davis and John C. Whitcomb (Baker). An outstanding work filled with the latest archaeological data. 542 pages.

Old Testament History, Charles F. Pfeiffer (Baker). A very valuable book containing much research made available on the popular level. Covers also the inter-biblical age. 640 pages.

The Heart of the Hebrew History, H.I. Hester (William Jewell Press). An older work but very clear and beautifully organized. Highly recommended. 331 pages.

The Heart of the New Testament, H.I. Hester (William Jewell Press). A continuation of Hester's work on the Old Testament. 351 pages. These two books should be in every library.

Bible History—The Old Testament, Alfred Edersheim (Eerdmans). This is an older work and thus dated in some respects. It is, however, filled with hundreds of valuable insights into the text of the Old Testament. Originally in 7 volumes, now available in one volume. Over 1,400 pages.

Studies in the Life of Christ, R.C. Foster (Baker). A masterpiece. Written in a beautiful style, devasting to liberal critical theories. 1,400 pages.

SURVEY OF BIBLE BOOKS

There are a number of excellent works that survey the individual books of the Bible, giving the cream of the information regarding these narratives, such as, authorship, background, people addressed, peculiarities, outline, main emphasis, etc. Here are some of these helpful tools.

Survey of the Bible, William Hendriksen (Baker). A useful work containing outlines, charts, interpretation principles, history, biblical books, etc. 497 pages.

An Introduction to the Old Testament, Edward J. Young (Eerdmans). A conservative though technical work. For the more advanced student. 456 pages.

New Testament Survey, Robert G. Gromacki (Baker). Background, analysis, and discussion of each book. 433 pages.

An Outlined Introduction to the Bible, John Waddey (Choate Publications). Presents in detail material on the books of the Bible—author, place, date, theme, unique features, lessons. 2 volumes on Old Testament completed; volume on New Testament in progress. Authored by an outstanding Christian writer. Highly recommended.

The Bible Book by Book, G. Coleman Luck (Moody). A handy little paperback for quick reference. Discusses: author, recipients, date, purpose, theme, key words/verses, outline. 253 pages. Some "premillennial" allusions.

Halley's Bible Handbook, H.H. Halley (Zondervan). An older work and somewhat dated, but still quite valuable for the average reader. Background, commentary, archaeology, maps, etc. 864 pages.

General Introduction to the Bible, Norman Geisler and William Nix (Moody). Structure and divisions of the Bible, canonicity, the apocrypha, translations, etc. 480 pages.

DICTIONARIES AND ENCYCLOPEDIAS

If there is an absolute "must" for the balanced library, it is the reference material to be found in the dictionaries and encyclopedias. We will list several: first, one volume works; the, multi-volume sets.

New Bible Dictionary, J.D. Douglas (Ed), (Eerdmans). Over 100 scholars, 2,300 articles. Latest archaeological discoveries. 1,407 pages. Some liberalism.

Zondervan Pictorial Bible Dictionary, Merrill C. Tenney (Ed), (Zondervan). 65 scholars, 5,000 entries, 700 photos. 973 pages. Watch for denominational bias.

New Smith's Bible Dictionary, Reuel Lemmons (Ed), (Doubleday). A revised edition of the original Smith's dictionary. Most of the contributors are scholars in the church of Christ. Good book for the average Christian. 441 pages.

Unger's Bible Dictionary, Merrill F. Unger (Ed), (Moody). Deals with archaeology, geography, biography, etc. 7,000 articles, 536 photos, 1,200 pages.

International Standard Bible Encyclopedia, James Orr (Ed), (Eerdmans). An older work thus somewhat dated, but more conservative that the later "Revised" edition (in progress). 5 volumes.

The Zondervan Pictorial Encyclopedia of the Bible, Merrill C. Tenney (Ed), (Zondervan). 238 scholars, 7,500 articles. The best set now available. 5 volumes.

Wycliffe Bible Encyclopedia, Charles Pfeiffer (Ed), (Moody). An outstanding work; generally conservative. Over a million words. 2 volumes; also available in an inexpensive paperback edition, 1 volume, unabridged.

CONCORDANCES

Strong's Exhaustive Concordance, James Strong (Baker). An indispensable tool from several angles. Contains all major English words in the Bible, plus Hebrew and Greek dictionaries. The numerical word code correlates with several other language tools.

Young's Analytical Concordance, Robert Young (Eerdmans). New edition accommodates some of the later versions. Almost 311,000 references, nearly 5,000,000 words.

COMMENTARIES

It is exceedingly difficult to find Bible commentaries that do not reflect sectarian bias. In using a commentary, therefore, it is quite important to know the religious persuasion of the author. In the majority of commentaries on the religious market today, information concerning God's plan of salvation, the church, New Testament worship, etc. will be erroneous. If this fact is recognized, many of these works can be used to great profit in other areas of biblical knowledge. Since we are addressing the average member of the church, we will make but a few recommendations in this area of library building.

One Volume Commentaries

Wycliffe Bible Commentary, Everett Harrison and Charles Pfeiffer (Eds), (Moody). An up-to-date phrase-by-phrase commentary on the entire Bible, authored by 48 top scholars. 1,525 pages.

The New Bible Commentary, Donald Guthrie, et. al. (Eerdmans). A very fine commentary, generally conservative. Outstanding introductions to the books. 1,310 pages.

Jamieson, Fausset and Brown's Commentary on the Whole Bible, (Zondervan). A popular reprint of an 1870's classic. Brief verse-by-verse exposition. 1,591 pages.

Commentary Sets (Whole Bible)

The Bible Commentary, F.C. Cook (Ed), (Baker). Critical and exegetical material on the whole Bible. Even though a century old, still quite valuable. 10 volumes.

Commentary on the Whole Bible, Matthew Henry (Revell). A monumental work that has been popular for two centuries. 6 volumes.

Clarke's Commentary, Adam Clarke (Abingdon). Clarke, a Methodist, spent some forty years in preparing this work. Old, but still useful. 3 large volumes.

Commentary Sets (New Testament)

Gospel Advocate Commentaries, various authors of the church of Christ (Gospel Advocate Co.). Popular, dependable, non-technical. 14 volumes.

Coffman's Commentary, James Burton Coffman (University Press). Easy-reading, thoroughly researched, drawing from many of the best modern sources. By a Christian author. 12 volumes. Highly recommended for the average student.

Barnes's Commentary on the New Testament, Albert Barnes (Baker). Though an older commentary, this work by a Presbyterian scholar is still valuable. Barnes is a much underrated commentator. 6 volumes; also available in a large, one volume edition (Kregel).

The People's New Testament With Notes, B.W. Johnson (Gospel Light). Brief explanatory notes on the New Testament text by a writer of the restoration movement. 1 volume.

LANGUAGE STUDIES

The New Testament is a book of words, and these words (the things "written") are inspired of God (II Timothy 3:16). Originally, the New Testament was composed in *koine* Greek, the language of the common man in the first century. The real New Testament, therefore, is the **Greek** Testament; all others are simply translations, and there is frequently something lost in translation, however minute it might be.

We are not suggesting that one must know Greek in order to live faithfully before Jehovah and reach heaven at last. We are saying that the best and richest teachers of the sacred

Scriptures are those who avail themselves of a study of the original biblical languages.

A study of the Greek New Testament is not always encouraged. There are some—a few college professors and preachers—who would discourage the average Christian from attempting to explore the original text, perhaps imagining that an exclusive grasp of the language gives them a mysterious sense of sacrosanct power over the uninitiated. There is absolutely no reason, though, why any careful student cannot avail himself of the many wonderful language tools now on the market and so "dig in" to some of the vast treasures of the Greek New Testament. The noted Greek grammarian, A. T. Robertson, once declared that "some knowledge of Greek is possible to all."

There are several books designed to get one started on this ambitious project.

"How To" Books

DO IT YOURSELF Hebrew and Greek—Everybody's Guide To The Language Tools, Edward W. Goodrick (Multnomah Press). This is an outstanding series of 22 systematic lessons in how to use the books available for studying the biblical languages.

The Minister and His Greek New Testament, A.T. Robertson (Baker). Rich lessons in some of the precious gems of New Testament Greek by one of the truly great grammarians.

How To Read The Greek New Testament, Guy N. Woods (Gospel Advocate). A simple introduction for those who wish to trace Greek words to their roots, define them, and observe their forms in sentence structure. Woods is an outstanding Christian scholar.

The Practical Use of the Greek New Testament, Kenneth Wuest (Moody). This Baptist scholar sometimes lets his "theology" get in the way of sound exegesis. That aside, this little book contains some valuable insights into grammatical studies. Thrilling reading.

Light From the Greek New Testament, Boyce Blackwelder (Warner Press). Another worthy volume dealing with nouns, verbs, prepositions, etc. Like others, though, watch him on "doctrinal" points.

Greek-English Testaments

Interlinear Greek-English New Testament, George R. Berry (Zondervan). Over and under lines of Greek and English, using the *Textus Receptus* with KJV in the margin, including a dictionary and synonym section. Other editions also available using different Greek text and other marginal translations.

Analytical Greek New Testament, Timothy and Barbara Friberg (Baker). Only the Greek text is given. Each word has a "grammatical tag" that is coded to an index card which gives the essential grammatical information about that term.

Concordance

Englishman's Greek Concordance of the New Testament, George Wigram (Zondervan). Alphabetically lists every word in the Greek New Testament. Numerically keyed to Strong's English concordance.

Dictionaries

A Greek-English Lexicon of the New Testament, J.H. Thayer (Baker). There are more modern lexicons available, but for the average person this will suffice. Word definitions and comment. One must know the Greek alphabet to use this book. Available in inexpensive paperback.

Expository Dictionary of New Testament Words, W.E. Vine (Riverside). An outstanding work; simple, fairly thorough, no knowledge of Greek required for use of this book.

Analytical Greek Lexicon, Revised, Harold Moulton (Zondervan). Every form of every Greek word is given, as well as the root form and grammatical analysis of the word. A number of helpful charts is included.

Commentaries

Word Pictures in the New Testament, A.T. Robertson (Baker). Verse by verse comments on the grammar. Easy for the English reader. 6 volumes.

Word Studies in the New Testament, Marvin Vincent (Eerdmans). Rich in background; verse-by-verse format. 4 volumes. A standard work.

Word Studies in the Greek New Testament, Kenneth Wuest (Eerdmans). Especially for those who do not read Greek but who wish to explore the wonderful world of the New Testament language. 3 volumes. Watch for his Baptist doctrine.

[Note: A word of caution—simply because we recommend a book generally, does not mean that we endorse everything in it.]

CONCLUSION

It has been said that fifty percent of all knowledge is knowing where to find the **other** fifty percent. One cannot constantly have a fresh remembrance of all that he has learned from the Bible. He can, though, if he has access to a good religious library, and knows how to efficiently use it, quickly research a variety of important themes and so become a delightfully more effective instructor. The lazy "teacher" (?) will never be a powerful influence for God.

Questions on Chapter 8

1. Why is there a great need for the study of "Christian evidences" today?

2. Using a Bible atlas, compare the size of the land of Canaan with that of the United States.

3. What is Bible "hermeneutics?"

4. How would you describe a book that takes a "conservative" approach to the Bible?

5. What areas of knowledge does a "Bible Introduction" address?

6. Look up the word "Corinth" in a Bible dictionary or encyclopedia. How would this information be helpful if you were discussing Paul's letter, First Corinthians?

7. What is a concordance?

8. In view of his "denominational bias," how would you expect Albert Barnes to view the "mode" of baptism?

9. What is *koine* Greek?

10. Complete this sentence: "Fifty percent of all knowledge is
    ...."

Suggestion: Make a "want list" of good Bible reference books.
Give the list to those who will be giving you gifts on special
occasions. Ask them to cooperate with you in this way in help-
ing build your library.

Chapter 9

ACCURATE BIBLICAL EXEGESIS

Hermeneutics is the science of correctly interpreting the Bible. More specifically, its design is to establish the principles, methods, and rules which are essential in ascertaining the meaning of the sacred text. The practical application of hermeneutical principles is known as "exegesis." The word "exegesis" derives from the Greek *exegeomai*, literally meaning, "to lead out." Exegesis is thus the attempt to bring out the meaning intended by the original author.

Let us, as we begin, remind ourselves of some important truths. First, the Bible was meant to be understood (Ephesians 5:17). It was not designed as a mystery book to baffle man! Second, interpretation of the Scriptures is not the exclusive prerogative of some priesthood or clergy; rather, it is both the right and obligation of every person to determine the meaning of the inspired text. Third, the scriptures were intended to have a definite meaning, to convey a specific message. No one, therefore, has the right to take an "existential" approach to the Bible thus suggesting, "This is what this passage means to me," as though one were permitted to seek from the verse what is personally satisfying to him, to the exclusion of its objective sense.

At this point, we would like to introduce a number of preliminary principles which will enable the student to approach the text of the Bible with exegetical soundness.

(1) **Context**—In considering the meaning of a particular

passage of scripture, one initially gives consideration to the context of the passage. How does this verse relate to the biblical book in which it occurs? In order to determine this, one should refresh his mind with the pertinent data regarding the scope of the book. He might read the book itself (if it is a brief one), or if that is not practical, consult a Bible Introduction (see chapter on "Tools") for this information. And then at least read the immediate section (chapter, etc.) in which the verse if found.

(2) Next, the student must determine **who is speaking** in this context. Is the author of the statement an inspired person or not? It must be noted that though the entire Bible is an inspired record, it nevertheless frequently contains statements from uninspired people. Isaiah 37:10-13 contains a letter from the pagan king of Assyria in which Jehovah is grossly blasphemed. In Job 4, there is the record of a "vision" which Eliphaz, Job's friend, allegedly had. By this device, he accuses the patriarch of grievous sins; a totally false charge! Obviously his testimony was not from God. There are even statements from Satan recorded in the Scriptures (Cf.: Matthew 4:6). It is thus vital to know who the speaker is.

(3) It is also essential to know **to whom the passage is addressed**. Christ once said, "But when they deliver you up, be not anxious how or what ye shall speak: for it shall be given you in that hour what ye shall speak. For it is not ye that speak, but the Spirit of your Father that speaketh in you" (Matthew 10:19, 20). That was a promise to the Lord's **miraculously endowed** disciples, and not to the world (or the church) generally. Again, Christ commanded: "....tarry ye in the city [Jerusalem], until ye be clothed with power from on high" (Luke 24:49). Is that a command for me? Of course not. The Lord was addressing the eleven apostles (Judas having died) in this context. When Peter commanded certain ones to "be baptized" (Acts 2:38), was he addressing saved people or lost people? He was speaking to those guilty of having crucified Jesus, who needed the "forgiveness of sins;" hence, to lost

souls. On the other hand, when the writer of Hebrews declared: "Take heed, brethren, lest haply there shall be in any one of you an evil heart of unbelief, in falling away from the living God" (3:12), he was directing his attention to the needs of **Christians** who were on the verge of apostasy. One absolutely must know to whom the instruction of a particular passage is being addressed.

(4) Another important principle that is sometimes quite crucial to a correct understanding of a verse is this: **how did the original recipients understand the instruction**? For example, we are told (John 8) that Christ engaged the Jews in a rather heated exchange. Near the end of the chapter, the Lord declared: "Before Abraham was born, I am" (8:58). What did the Savior mean by that? Was he simply claiming a **created** existence prior to Abraham (e.g., an angel), as the Jehovah's Witnesses suggest, or was he arguing for an **eternal** existence (as implied by the present tense form, *ego eimi*, "I am")? His audience obviously understood him to identify with the latter, for they immediately picked up stones to execute him for the crime of blasphemy, that is, claiming the nature of eternal deity.

When Christ delivered his famous Olivet Discourse (Matthew 24:4ff), he spoke of those who would "flee unto the mountains," etc., due to an impending tribulation. How did the Christians of that day understand the Lord's admonition? Did they envision a 20th century nuclear holocaust, as the dispensational premillennialists contend? Hardly. The evidence indicates that they interpreted the Savior's warning of the impending destruction of Jerusalem. Eusebius notes: "The whole body, however, of the church at Jerusalem, having been commanded by a divine revelation, given to men of approved piety there before the war [of 70 A.D.], removed from the city, and dwelt at a certain town beyond the Jordan, called Pella" (*Ecclesiastical History*, III, VI).

(5) Additionally, if possible, one should attempt to **determine the circumstances** under which a narrative was written. Was there any special historical or problematic situation

involved? This is quite important, for instance, in studying I Corinthians, chapter 7, where Paul advises against marriage. How does one account for such advice in view of the general principle that it "is not good for man to be alone" (Genesis 2:18)? The answer is simple. Paul's instruction was in view of a "present distress," (7:26) that is, a persecution, under which those Christians were laboring, when marital relationships would make fidelity to God more difficult to maintain.

What does Paul mean when he cautions: "Let no man rob you of your prize by a voluntary humility and worshipping of the angels...." (Colossians 2:18). This passage, along with others in the same epistle, can only be fully appreciated in light of a certain proto-gnostic, Judaic heresy that was being advocated among the saints in Colossae. The apostle's teaching was thus flavored by the needs of that ancient situation. [For a discussion of the probable elements of this false philosophy, see William Barclay's material in his commentary on this letter.]

(6) It is sometimes important to **be familiar with certain geographical or topographical data** relative to a scriptural text. In studying the Lord's parable about the Good Samaritan, it is helpful to learn that the 4,000 foot descent from Jerusalem to Jericho is a lonely and dangerous trail. The eighteen mile trip would have taken about six hours and the road was an infamous habitat for robbers. In his magnificent volume, *Studies In The Life Of Christ* (Baker, 1971), R.C. Foster has an entire chapter entitled, "The Influence of the Weather Upon the Ministry of Jesus." Note, for instance, the teaching ministry of Christ within the protective accommodation of Solomon's porch in the temple during the cold winter, rainy period of December (feast of the dedication) as indicated in John 10:22, 23. These are points facilitating good exegesis that many folks never think about.

(7) Occasionally, it is necessary to **determine the correct text** (from several manuscript variations) of a particular passage. One observes, for instance, that in the American Stan-

dard Version footnotes, there are these frequent notations: "Some ancient authorities read...." The better critical commentaries will discuss the manuscript evidence for the text. Bruce Metzger's work, *A Textual Commentary On The Greek New Testament*, (United Bible Societies, 1971), is quite helpful in this regard.

Having considered some preliminary points which are preparatory to sound exegesis, we are ready to approach the text itself. I have found the material of William Hendriksen (*Survey of the Bible*, Baker, 1976) quite helpful in this area. I submit several of his suggestions with my own adaptations.

(1) The **word order** of a sentence, as it appears in the original language, may suggest some important truths. In Greek, the normal order is subject first, predicate second. The verb is generally followed by its object. If the order is changed, the author is emphasizing a special point. For instance, the Greek of John 3:16 reads, "For **so loved** God the world...." There is stress upon the divine love. In John 10:11 the common translation reads: "I am the good shepherd...." The Greek idiom is: "I am the shepherd, the good...." There is a contrast being emphasized between Christ and the Jewish leaders, who pretended to be shepherds of Jehovah's people, but had miserably failed in that responsibility.

(2) Next, the exegete, being aware that the words of the Bible are from God, will want to **take careful note of the terms used** in the passage. The use of a Greek lexicon (dictionary—see chapter on "Tools") will be a necessity for this type of detailed work. One may attempt to determine the "root" meaning of the principle terms. Especially, though, he must ascertain the word's meaning as used in the New Testament. Moreover, attention must be paid to grammatical forms of nouns, verbs, participles, etc. Frequently there are volumes of truth hidden away in grammatical distinctions. We will not linger on this point here for we intend to discuss it in greater detail in the chapter to follow.

(3) The keen Bible student must keep a sharp watch for

words that are used in an unusual sense. The Bible absolutely abounds with a variety of literary devices which are effectively employed to convey truth, Let us note a sampling of these.

Jesus frequently spoke in **parables** (Cf.: Matthew 13), the design of which was either to conceal the truth from those who would abuse it (Matthew 13:13f), or to more clearly reveal it to those honest souls who would profit from it. By means of the **simile**, certain Pharisees were "like unto whited sepulchers" (Matthew 23:27). Christ was using **metaphors** when he said, "This is my body....this is my blood" (Matthew 26:26-28), he was not suggesting transubstantiation. Note Paul's use of the **allegory** of the two women (representing the two covenants) in Galatians 4. By a figure known as **metonomy**, the Spirit stands for the instruction he brought in I Corinthians 12:13, so, literally, it is by the message of the Spirit that one is led to be immersed into the body of Christ (Cf.: Ephesians 5:26). Similarly, "Moses and the prophets" in Luke 16:31, by metonomy, stands for the Old Testament law. By means of the **synecdoche** (part put for the whole, etc.), one item of the plan of salvation is made to stand for the entire plan, e.g., being justified by **faith**, we have peace with God (Romans 5:1). Certainly such requirements as "repentance" and "baptism" are not excluded (Cf.: Acts 2:38; 11:18; I Peter 3:21). And so, there are hundreds of figures of speech in the Scriptures which must be carefully noted by the diligent student. E.W. Bullinger's, *Figures of Speech Used in the Bible* (Baker, 1968, pp 1104), is probably the most exhaustive treatise on this theme.

(4) The Scriptures contain numerous examples of **synonymous parallelism** and a recognition of this can frequently aid in the interpretation of Bible verses. God, through the prophet Hosea, asked: "How shall I give thee up, Ephraim? How shall I deliver thee, Israel?" (11:8). In this context, Ephraim is simply a term used for the northern kingdom of Israel. Notice the parallel reasoning in Romans 10:16. "But they have not all **obeyed** the gospel. For Isaiah saith, Lord, who **hath be-**

lieved our report?" (KJV). It is clear from the comparison that genuine believing is obeying!

We would also suggest that comparative Bible study is a most valuable procedure for accurate exegesis, but we will reserve a more complete discussion of this subject until chapter 11.

(5) Finally, we would emphasize that there is no virtue in exegesis for exegesis' sake. One must ask: "What does the passage mean in my life? How can I appropriate this information so as to make me a better person?" The point is, the Bible must be studied for the **practical** benefits derived from it. The sacred Book is designed to mold us into the image of Him who, as a forerunner for us, has entered heaven already!

Now that we have looked at some of the principles for accurate interpretation, let's put our knowledge to work and do some real exegesis on one of the most familiar passages of the Bible, John 3:16—"For God so loved the world, that he gave his only begotten Son, that whosoever believeth on him should not perish, but have eternal life."

PRELIMINARY INFORMATION

This marvelous verse is, of course, a part of the larger context of this entire book. The design of John's gospel record is expressed near the end of the document. The book's aim is "that ye may believe that Jesus is the Christ, the Son of God; and that believing ye may have life in his name" (20:31). John 3:16 speaks to this very issue!

Second, John 3:16 is a continuation, either by the Lord [Cf.: Godet, *Commentary on the Gospel of St. John*, T. & T. Clark, 1890, II, pp 68, 69], or by the apostle [Westcott, *The Gospel According to John*, Murray, 1908, I, pp 87, 88], of Christ's conversation with Nicodemus regarding the "new birth." It is thus clear that the "belief" which leads to "eternal life" is not independent of the new birth process!

Third, John 3:16 is introduced by the conjunction "for" [*gar* in Greek], which is employed to explain a foregoing statement. In this case, a historical situation from the time of Moses had just been introduced. In the wilderness of Sinai, Israel murmured against Jehovah and the Lord sent fiery serpents among them as punishment. When the people cried for deliverance, God had Moses fashion a brazen serpent and set it upon a standard. Those, who "looked" upon it in faith were spared death (Cf.: Numbers 21:4-9). The incident of the serpent was a "type" of the death of Christ and our deliverance through him. Note the "even so" terminology of John 3:14. As the serpent was "lifted up," so must the Lord be "lifted up" on the cross (Cf.: John 12:32). The object of all of this was that "whosoever believeth may in him [*en auto*—dative case of location] have eternal life" (15). This background leads up to John 3:16.

TEXTUAL ANALYSIS

God so loved—The term "God" here denotes the Father. "Loved" is from the Greek *agapao*, a word suggesting genuine interest, determined dedication. It is the sacrificial love that acts in the welfare of others even in the face of hostility. It is the kind of love that motivates our response to the will of Jehovah (Cf.: W.E. Vine, *Expository Dictionary*, III, p. 21). We love because he first loved us (I John 4:19). The extent of the divine love is underscored by the use of the term "so" (marking intensity). God loved, not passively, but actively; givingly!

The World—The Greek word for "world" is *cosmos*, literally denoting the orderly universe created by God. In a more limited sense it is used of the earth (Mark 16:15). Here, by means of the figure known as metonomy (the container being put for the contents), it means the people of the world. The term thus emphasizes the **universal** love of God. The word is in direct opposition to the Calvinistic notion that Jehovah, before the world's foundation, elected only a certain number of people to be saved. The Lord wants **all** to be saved (Cf.: John 1:29; I Timothy 2:6; Titus 2:11; II Peter 3:9).

That he gave—Giving is characteristic of God (Cf.: Acts 14:17; 17:25; James 1:17), and His greatest gift, of course, was that of His Son (Cf.: Isaiah 9:6; II Corinthians 9:15). Even when a gift is available, though, someone must be willing to **receive** it. There must be concurrence between the will of the giver and the will of the benefactor. Observe this example: God **gave** Israel the city of Jericho (Joshua 6:2), yet they could not possess the city until after they obeyed the Lord's will for **taking** it (Cf.: Hebrews 11:30). Similarly, God gave His Son, but the Son must be received (John 1:11) in loving obedience (Hebrews 5:9).

His only begotten Son—"Only begotten" renders the Greek *monogenes*, found nine times in the New Testament (five of these of Christ—John 1:14, 18; 3:16, 18; I John 4:9). The term derives from two roots, *monos* (only, alone) and *genos* (race, stock). In the contexts where it is used of Jesus, it suggests that He is "unique in kind." There is no other being in heaven or on earth like Him—God-man. [Note: this would exclude Christ from the **angel** class, contrary to the assertions of the "Jehovah's Witnesses."]

That whosoever believeth on him—Again, "whosoever" reveals the universal scope of God's redemptive plan (Cf.: Revelation 22:17). The verb "believe" in Greek is *pisteuo*. Actually, here it is a present tense participle, literally, therefore, the "keeping on believing ones" [continuing action]. Biblical faith involves the acceptation of historical facts, the disposition to trust the object of the faith, and a willingness to be obedient to divine requirements. That faith includes obedience is plainly evidenced by John 3:36 (ASV). "He that **believeth** on the Son hath eternal life; but he that **obeyeth not** the Son shall not see life, but the wrath of God abideth on him."

Should not perish—The Greek word for "perish" is *apol-*

106

lumi, a very strong word meaning "to utterly destroy." The term does not suggest annihilation, as materialists contend. This is the word used to describe the miserable condition of the prodigal son when separated from his father; in that state, the son was "lost" (*apollumi*). As W.E. Vine notes, "the idea is not extinction but ruin, loss, not of being, but of well-being" (*Expository Dictionary*, I, p. 302).

But have eternal life—Eternal life is not merely eternal existence, for the wicked will exist eternally, but they will not enjoy eternal life. Eternal life is the exact opposite of everlasting death. The final abode of the wicked is called the "second death" (Revelation 20:6, 14). Since death always denotes a separation of some sort, the final death is obviously the ultimate separation from God (Cf.: Matthew 7:23; 25:41; II Thessalonians 1:9). Conversely, eternal life is everlasting **communion with God**.

John 3:16 is truly a wonderful passage. I have given it a more exhaustive analysis in my small tract, *The Truth About John 3:16*, Apologetics Press, 1981.

CONCLUSION

Scholarly Bible exegesis is a thrill beyond comparison; it is "meat" of which many know not. With determination, some good working tools, and an honest heart, any Christian can become a rich student and superior teacher of the Word of God.

Questions on Chapter 9

1. Define "hermeneutics." Define "exegesis."

2. What is an "existential" approach to the Bible?

3. In what type of "reference work" might one find a discussion of the theme of the biblical books?

4. Why is it important to know "who" is speaking in a given context?

5. Read John 14:26 and determine specifically to whom this promise is made.

6. What was the significance of Christ's claim, "Before Abraham was born, I am."?

7. In I Corinthians 7, Paul advised against getting married. What special circumstances qualify this admonition?

8. In doing "word studies," the most important task of the student is to discover how the word is used in the _____ _____.

9. Give an example of the figure of speech known as "metonymy."

10. How does John 3:16 tie in with Old Testament.history?

11. Discuss the meaning of "love" in John 3:16.

12. Can you demonstrate that "believeth" in John 3:16 is not an affirmation of salvation by "faith alone."

13. Define "eternal life."

Chapter 10

THE STUDY OF BIBLICAL WORDS

The Bible is a book of words. It is said that there are 8,674 words in the Hebrew Text of the Old Testament and 5,624 Greek words in the New Testament. Since the Bible is the verbally inspired Word of God (II Timothy 3:16), and by its words spiritual life is obtained (Matthew 4:4; James 1:21), it is obvious that no person who is really interested in the eternal welfare of his soul can afford to neglect a careful study of the words of sacred Scripture.

A study of Bible words can, and should, be approached from several different angles. In this chapter, we will consider three important concepts: (1) word etymology; (2) grammatical form; and, (3) context.

ETYMOLOGY

Etymology is that branch of "word science" that has to do with the origin and development of words. The investigation of a word's root form may be very helpful in obtaining a full and rich meaning of certain passages. For example, the Hebrew words *kopher*, *kippurim*, and *kapporeth*, which are rendered by the English terms "ransom," "redemptions" or "atonements," and "Mercy-seat," are all derived from the root *kaphar*, which means "to cover." The words suggest that redemption or atonement is accomplished by a "covering" of sin. The meaning is this: when one, through obedient faith responds to the Will of God, his sins are covered by the blood of Christ. In the Old Testament, of course, the blood of animal sacrifices typified the redemptive death of the Lord.

In the New Testament, numerous Greek words have great etymological significance. The word for "church" (*ekklesia*) derives from the roots *ek*, a preposition meaning "out of," and *klesis*, "a calling," hence, a calling out of. It thus denotes a spiritual body of people who have been called by the gospel (II Thessalonians 2:14) out of the world (Cf.: John 15:19; Colossians 1:13) into a holy relationship with Jehovah (II Corinthians 6:17, 18). Or consider the word translated "bishop" in our English Bibles. It is from the Greek term *episkopos*; the root forms are *epi* (upon) and *skopeo* (to look or watch; Cf.: our word "scope"). The New Testament term thus denotes a certain class of men, possessing Spirit-given qualifications (Acts 20:28; I Timothy 3:1ff; Titus 1:5ff), who are appointed to oversee or supervise the business of local churches of Christ.

In Philippians 1:20, Paul spoke of the "earnest expectation" which he had in Christ. The Greek word is *apokaradokia* from three roots: *apo*, "from," *kara*, "the head," and *dokeo*, "to look, to watch." The term denotes one who turns his attention away from distractions and concentrates upon an object of great interest. In this context it reveals the intensity of Paul's religious fervor.

The New Testament contains hundreds of thrilling examples of these rich nuggets of truth tucked away in the Greek text of scripture. For the average church member, a good book like W.E. Vine's *Expository Dictionary of New Testament Words*, can be a valuable tool in determining the original significance of New Testament words.

It must be recognized, however, that words, as they travel across several generations of time, can loose their etymological meaning and take on a new emphasis. The careful Bible student must therefore ask: does this word retain its etymological significance, or has it adopted a "derivative" meaning? In other words, what did the word actually mean at the time it was employed by the biblical writer? A failure to recognize this fact has led to some rather serious doctrinal errors.

Originally, the word *kolazo* meant to "prune" or to "cut off," but by the time of the New Testament age, the word conveyed the idea of "punish" (Cf.: Acts 4:21; II Peter 2:9). It is, therefore, a serious blunder to forsake this New Testament **derivative** meaning and revert to an earlier usage. This is precisely what the Watchtower Witnesses have done in the case of Matthew 25:46. There, the Lord speaks of the wicked entering into eternal "punishment" (*kolasis*), whereas the Watchtower translation of the Bible, in attempting to avoid the idea of punishment (which implies consciousness), renders the term "everlasting cutting-off," thus hinting at the total extinction of the unrighteous.

Similarly, even though the word *psallo* denoted "plucking" in the era of classical Greek (500-300 B.C.), later, in the Koine period (300 B.C.-300 A.D.), *psallo* was already being used to simply denote singing. By the time of the Byzantine era (300-500 A.D.) and in modern Greek, the term had come to signify "to sing" or "to chant" exclusively. All of the available evidence indicates that in the New Testament the word denoted only singing, or perhaps, **figuratively** plucking the strings of the **heart** (Cf.: Ephesians 5:19), but not mechanical accompaniment. Note the testimony of W.E. Vine, a denominational scholar, in this respect: "The word *psallo* originally meant to play a stringed instrument with the fingers, or to sing with the accompaniment of a harp. Later, however, and in the New Testament, it came to signify simply to praise without the accompaniment of an instrument" (*I Corinthians—Local Church Problems*, Zondervan, 1951, p. 191).

The Greek word *pneuma* derives from the root *pneo* ("to breathe"), and originally it meant "breath." In the New Testament, though, it has come to mean: (1) The Holy Spirit, the third Person in the Godhead, (I Timothy 4:1); (2) The human personality, that part of man which "knows" (I Corinthians

2:11); (3) A disposition, attitude, or way of life, e.g., John the Baptizer came in the "spirit" of Elijah (Luke 1:17). The Watchtower organization is wrong, therefore, in assigning "breath" as the meaning of *pneuma* in the New Testament.

GRAMMATICAL MODE

A second factor that must be considered in the study of words is that of syntax. In studying syntax, one is dealing with the grammatical principles of the language in which the document was originally written. It is important to remember that the function of grammar is not to determine the laws of language; rather, it merely explains how that language was employed by the people who originally used it.

In the study of syntax (the relationship of words to one another), one will ask, for instance: is the term with which I am dealing a noun, verb, adjective, preposition, etc.? If it is a noun, is it singular or plural? Of what gender is it? In what case is it found? If one is analyzing a verb, he will want to know such things as: what is the voice of this verb? The tense? The mood? All of these factors contribute to the understanding of a term in the sentence in which it is found. Let us note some examples.

In John 1:12, 13, the apostle affirms that as many as received Christ, to them he gave the right to become children of God, even to them who continue to believe on his name. Then, describing these children of God negatively, he declares: "who were born, not of **blood**...." It is important to note that the term "blood" here is actually a plural word (Cf.: ASV fn), and the thought is this: whereas one was constituted a child of God under the Mosaic covenant by virtue of this Hebrew parentage (suggested by "bloods"—cf.: Paul's phrase, "a Hebrew of Hebrews"—Philippians 3:5), such was not to be the case under the new system. Under the Christian regime that spiritual family relationship is accomplished by means of a

new birth (John 3:3-5).

In Ephesians 2:8, Paul wrote: "For by grace have ye been saved through faith; and that not of yourselves, it is the gift of God." Due to a misunderstanding of this passage, some have contended that one need not exercise personal faith in God in order to be saved; rather, faith, it is claimed, is a "gift" that one passively receives. That is a misunderstanding of this verse. It would be helpful to note that "faith" in this passage is a **feminine** gender form, whereas, "gift" is a **neuter** gender form. The "gift" referred to in the verse, therefore, is not faith. The gift is salvation, implied in the context by the verbal form "saved." (For elaboration of this point, see Clinton Lockhart's, *Principles of Interpretation*, pp. 85, 86).

Or consider the fact that some argue, on the basis of Galatians 3:26, that salvation is solely a matter of faith in Christ, and that baptism is not included as a condition of salvation. This claim is carelessly made: "Paul says that we are children of God by faith in Christ, and that settles it." The truth is, though, the apostle is not here discussing "faith in Christ," as though "Christ" were the object of one's faith. Had such been true, the name "Christ" would have been written in the **accusative** case. But it is not. An examination of the Greek text reveals that in this passage "Christ" is in the **dative** case, the case of location. The apostle is thus discussing the realm or sphere wherein salvation takes place; it is "in Christ." He then proceeds to inform us as to how one enters that relationship. "For [an explanatory term] as many of you as were baptized into Christ did put Christ on" (vs. 27).

Or consider some of the grammatical truths connected with verbs. In New Testament Greek, as in English, verbs have **tense**, but the tense has more to do with the type of action under consideration than with time (time is secondary). Has the action in view been completed? It is on-going, etc.? A comprehension of these matters can add much meaning to one's study of the sacred text.

When Peter spoke of his impending death (II Peter 1:14),

he alluded to the fact that the Lord had "signified" such unto him. The verb "signified" is an aorist tense form and this indicates that the apostle is specifically thinking of that event in John 21:18, 19, wherein our Lord "signified" by what manner of death Peter should glorify God. In Matthew's gospel account, we are informed that Herod inquired of the chief priests and scribes as to where Christ would be born (Matthew 2:4). The verb "inquired" is an imperfect tense form, and this reveals that the king had **repeatedly** made such inquiries in his frantic efforts to locate baby Jesus! Paul expressed surprise that his Galatian brethren were so soon "removed" (KJV) from their holy calling (Galatians 1:6); actually, though, the Greek verb is in the present tense, indicating that their apostasy was **presently in progress**! The present tense form "committeth adultery" in Matthew 19:9 clearly shows that the unscripturally divorced and remarried person is committing adultery on a sustained basis, that is, living a life of adulterous intercourse. A consideration of tense forms is thus vitally important in sound biblical exegesis.

Verbs also have **voice**, which indicates how the action is related to the subject of the sentence. The **active** voice represents the subject as acting, the **passive** voice represents the subject as being acted upon, and the **middle** voice suggests the subject is acting in some way in reference to itself. Here are some examples of the value of this knowledge.

The King James Version, in Hebrews 7:26, describes Christ as "separate from sinners." Is the Lord's purity being stressed? No, not in this case. The Greek verb is actually a **passive** form (Cf.: ASV), and thus, in this context, is an allusion to Christ's ascension, at which point he was "made higher than the heavens."

In Acts 18:5, there is the record of Silas and Timothy coming from Macedonia and joining Paul in Corinth. The inspired writer informs us that on this occasion, Paul was, according to the common version, "pressed in spirit." But what does that mean? The better Greek text, with a **middle voice** form, indicates that the apostle "held himself to the word," that is, on this occasion he refrained from his usual trade of tent-making and confined himself solely to preaching the gospel. A knowledge of the verbal voice makes an otherwise obscure phrase wonderfully clear. It is quite important to give careful attention to the grammatical details of the Bible.

CONTEXT

In an earlier chapter we spoke of the necessity of respecting the context of biblical passages. This is also true of words. The contextual setting is the most important aspect of word studies, for the **special use** of a word, in a given context, can overrule both etymology and grammar. Let us look at several examples.

In Matthew 3:10, Jesus declared that "every tree which bringeth not forth good fruit **is cut down** [present tense], and cast into the fire." Though the present tense form is used, the context shows that the Judgment Day is in view, and the present is figuratively employed to stress the **certainty** of that future event. Similarly, Jesus told his disciples, "The Son of man **is delivered** [present tense, even though affirming a future event] into the hands of men...." (Mark 9:31). The divine plan cannot be thwarted!

In Romans 8:16, we are told that the "Spirit **itself** [neuter gender in Greek] bears witness with our spirit." Even though the pronoun is in the neuter gender, the context clearly demonstrates that the "Holy Spirit," a divine **person**, is in view and the neuter is simply grammatical agreement with the neuter term *pneuma* [Spirit]. On the other hand, inspired writers sometimes allowed contextual [doctrinal] considerations to dominate grammatical precision. John's gospel account states: "But when the Comforter is come, whom I will send unto you from the Father, even the Spirit [*pneuma*—neuter] of truth, who proceedeth from the Father, he [*ekeinos*—mascu-

115

line] shall bear witness of me" (15:26). Normally, the pronoun referring to the Spirit should be neuter, but the writer's affirmation of the Spirit's personality overrides the grammar here.

Additionally, it must be stressed that the same word can have widely different meanings in different contexts. For instance, the Greek word *presbuteros* is translated "elder." The term is used, though, in a variety of ways. It can denote merely those who are advanced in age (Acts 2:17). It is employed of Israel's ancestors (Hebrews 11:2); of members of the Jewish Sanhedrin (Matthew 16:21); of heavenly beings around the throne of God (Revelation 4:4); or, of leaders in the church (I Timothy 5:17). Clearly, the context must determine the usage of this word in these respective settings.

We have spoken of the word *ekklesia*, usually rendered "church" in our common versions. Most often it denotes that body of the Lord's "called out" people—sometimes in an assembled capacity (I Corinthians 14:34), or in a local (I Corinthians 1:2), geographical (Acts 9:31), or universal (Matthew 16:18) sense. Beyond that, however, the term is used of the congregation of Israel in the wilderness (Acts 7:38), or of the unruly mob at Ephesus (Acts 19:32), or of a city council (Acts 19:39).

Consider the term *peirazo*, which can mean either "to tempt" or "to try, test." James states that God "tempts no man" (1:13). How does one harmonize this statement with the biblical affirmation elsewhere that the Lord "tried" [from *peirazo*] Abraham (Cf.: Hebrews 11:17; Genesis 22:1)? The harmonization is obviously made on the basis of contextual differences. James used the word "tempt" in the sense of "soliciting to evil, attempting to ensnare." God never does that; such would be contrary to his holy nature. On the other hand, though the writer of Hebrews employs the same term, he does so with a different meaning. Jehovah "proved" or "tested" the father of the Hebrew nation. There is no conflict when the context is respected.

116

The Greek word for "dead" is *nekros*, but the entire story is not told just in the word. One may be dead physically as a result of the spirit's departure from the body (James 2:26). A person can be physically alive, but "dead" in sin (i.e., spiritually separated from God—Ephesians 2:1, 5), or he can, through conversion, be "dead" to sin (i.e., to the love and habitually unrestrained practice of it—Romans 6:11).

Our word "kingdom" is from the Greek *basileia*, which basically denotes "sovereignty, royal power, dominion, etc." Contextually, though, *basileia* is used in a host of ways in the New Testament. It may be used of: (1) an earthly political power (Matthew 4:8); (2) God's reign among the ancient Jews (Matthew 21:43); (3) of that spiritual body, the church, which has been called out of darkness into light (Colossians 1:13); (4) of the future abode of the saints, heaven itself (II Timothy 4:18). Again, the point of all this is that the totality of truth does not turn solely upon etymology, nor even grammar, but upon the entire biblical picture regarding a word.

The study of Bible words is truly a thrilling endeavor, but it requires skill, some good language tools, common sense, patience, and an honesty that wants above all else to deal accurately with Jehovah's sacred Word.

Questions on Chapter 10

1. List three important ways of viewing the "words" of the Bible.

2. Define "etymology."

3. Using a book like Vine's *Expository Dictionary*, look up the word "helpeth" (Romans 8:26). What are the root components of that term?

4. What fallacy have the Jehovah's Witnesses committed with reference to the use of *kolasis* in Matthew 25:46?

5. What is the "gift" mentioned in Ephesians 2:8?

6. What does the present tense form "committeth adultery" (Matthew 19:9) indicate?

7. What is the most important aspect of "word studies"?

8. How is the personality of the Holy Spirit emphasized in John 15:26?

9. If God never "tempts" man, how does one explain Genesis 22:1 (KJV)?

10. Show some of the ways that the word "kingdom" is used in the New Testament.

Chapter 11

COMPARATIVE BIBLE STUDY

In Psalm 119:160, the inspired writer declares: "The sum of thy word is truth" (ASV). In the Hebrew text of the Old Testament, the term rendered "sum" is *rosh*, which has several possible meanings depending upon the contextual setting. Here, however, the sense appears to be the "sum" or the "total" components of an object. The affirmation of the passage would thus be that the word of Jehovah is true in all of its individual parts.

The various books of the Bible were designed to eventually compose the whole of the sacred volume. And, as we have repeatedly stressed, since the Scriptures were ultimately authored by God, the implication is that the different portions of the divine document will not conflict or clash with one another; rather, they will complement each other.

It is, therefore, very important, in studying a text of scripture, to determine if there is biblical information elsewhere that will enhance one's understanding of the passage currently engaging his attention. It will be in his interest to gather all of the available data on the subject, lay them side by side, and thus attempt to see the total picture. This is called "comparative Bible study."

There are several tools that one may use in assembling his material. Center-column references will frequently direct attention to parallel portions of scripture. One needs, therefore, a good center-column reference Bible. A concordance (which lists Bible words with their references) can be quite helpful. Articles in Bible dictionaries and encyclopedias will cite related material, as will good commentaries. (See chapter on "Tools" for specific works.) If one is studying in the four gospel accounts, a parallel column arrangement, such as found in A.T. Robertson's *Harmony of the Gospels* (Harper & Row), can be very useful.

Comparative Bible study is valuable from a number of different vantage points. Let us give attention to several of these.

(1) Comparative Bible study has an **apologetic** value. "Apologetics" is the science of defending the faith. In this instance, we are speaking of interrelated biblical evidence that argues for the divine origin of the Bible.

In 1790, William Paley published his famous work, *Horae Paulinae, or the Truth of the Scripture History of St. Paul evinced by a Comparison of the Epistles which bear his Name with the Acts of the Apostles, and with one another*. Somewhat later, Professor J.J. Blunt of Cambridge authored his book, *Undesigned Coincidences*, which addressed the Old Testament in much the same manner as Paley's effort had the New Testament. Both of these volumes proposed to show that the intricate details of related Bible events were so subtle, and yet so precise (with never the trace of a "slip"), that it is impossible that they could have been produced without divine oversight. Let us note a couple of examples.

In the New Testament, we learn that myrrh and aloes were employed in the embalming of bodies, and that it took about one hundred pounds for one person (John 19:39). Furthermore, we recall that Egypt was quite famous for its embalming techniques (Cf.: Genesis 50:3, 26). We would conclude, therefore, that Egypt would require great supplies of these spices. Is there any incidental evidence that such was the case. Indeed. In Genesis 37:25, one notices a casual reference to a caravan that was journeying down into/or to Egypt—its cargo, "spicery and balm and myrrh." The pieces lock together as in a puzzle. And this is not a mere coincidence; it happens literally hundreds of times in the inspired accounts. Consider this New Testament example.

According to the book of Philemon, Onesimus, a slave, had run away from his master, Philemon, and made his way to Rome. There, he met the apostle Paul, who converted him to Christ. The question is, where did Philemon live? The book does not say. But if we do some biblical "detective" work, we can figure it out. According to Paul's letter to the Colossians (4:10), Onesimus was a native of the city of Colossae. Since he had fled from Philemon, we may tentatively conclude that Philemon was also a citizen of Colossae. But is there any way to cross-check our deduction. Yes there is. In Philemon 1:2, we are informed that Philemon lived in the same city as a brother named Archippus. Well, where did Archippus live? According to Colossians 4:12 he lived in Colossae. Hence, Philemon lived in Colossae!

Now these facts may seem rather trivial to the superficial student, but they are highly significant. They demonstrate that the biblical documents mesh together with an amazing accuracy that cannot be explained on the basis of strictly human authorship.

(2) Comparative Bible study aids in **explaining the meaning** of certain words or phrases in the sacred text. For instance, concerning Moses' birth the scripture states: "the woman conceived, and bare a son: and when she saw him that he was a goodly child, she hid him three months" (Exodus 2:2). What does the expression "goodly child" mean? A comparison of this passage with Stephen's observation in Acts 7:20 is illuminating. Stephen says that Moses was "exceedingly fair" (ASV), or, as the Greek more literally has it, he was "beautiful before God." It is an indication of the Lord's estimation of this child (Cf.: Jonah 3:3 ASVfn), with perhaps a hint of the prophet's divine mission.

According to Luke's account, the Lord once said: "If any man cometh unto me, and hateth not his own father, and mother, and wife, and children, and brethren, and sisters, yea, and his own life also, he cannot be my disciple" (14:26). Now that passage, isolated from its parallels, is rather difficult. When we compare, though, Matthew's account, we find the apostle recording these words: "He that loveth father or mother **more than me** is not worthy of me...." (10:37). If one thus "sums up" these complementary verses, it readily becomes apparent that Luke's "hate" for one's family is equivalent to **loving them less** than one loves the Son of God!

Here is another illustration. In Acts 3:19, after he had performed the notable miracle on the lame man, Peter commanded: "Repent ye therefore, and turn again [the KJV passive form "be converted" is incorrect], that your sins may be blotted out...." When I read this remarkable verse I might well ask myself, "What does 'turn again' mean?" The solution is to be found by comparing this passage with Acts 2:38 where the same apostle commanded his audience to "repent ye, and be baptized every one of you in the name of Jesus Christ unto the remission of your sins...." Note the parallel:

Repentance + Baptism = Remission of Sins
Repentance + Turning = Sins Blotted Out

Upon observing the two verses together, it becomes quite clear that one actually "turns" to the Savior at the point of his baptism!

(3) Comparative Bible study can frequently considerably expand the student's information on a given subject. Notice the following interesting comparisons.

Eve, in attempting to rationalize her sinful conduct, said: "The serpent beguiled me, and I did eat" (Genesis 3:13). Paul, in a comment on this, declares that "the serpent beguiled Eve **in his craftiness**" (II Corinthians 11:3). Moreover, the apostle affirms that because of this beguiling influence, "the woman **hath fallen into transgression** [the perfect tense underscores the abiding effect of the sin]" (I Timothy 2:14). Finally, though, woman **can be saved through her childbearing**, if continuing in faith, love and sanctification with sobriety (I Timothy 2:15).

In Genesis 39, there is the wonderful story of the spiritual young Joseph who resisted the advances of Potiphar's wife. As a consequence, "Joseph's master took him, and put him into the prison, the place where the king's prisoners were **bound**" (20). A center-column reference directs my attention to Psalm 105:18 and there I learn that "his feet they hurt with fetters: he was laid in chains of iron." I would have missed some real richness by failing to observe that related reference.

In Exodus 2:11 we read: "And it came to pass in those days, when Moses was **grown up**, that he went out unto his brethren, and looked on their burdens...." Exactly how grown up was he? Stephen says that he "was well nigh forty years old" (Acts 7:23). When the prophet sought to deliver his brethren by the signs which had been given him by God, Pharaoh's magicians became his competitors (Exodus 7:11). In an obvious allusion to this incident, Paul declares that "Jannes and Jambres withstood Moses" (II Timothy 3:8). These names were common in Jewish tradition, respectively meaning "to seduce" and "to incite," thus illustrating the effect of their deceptions upon Pharaoh.

When Jesus came to the city of Capernaum, a centurion approached him, saying, "Lord, my servant is lying in the house sick of the palsy, grievously tormented" (Matthew 8:6). A comparison of Luke 7:2 reveals some other interesting details. First, the servant was "dear" to him, that is, highly honored. Second, this Gentile's request was conveyed to the Lord by means of some Jewish elders (an evidence of their regard for the centurion). Third, it was an emergency situation for the servant was "at the point of death." Much of the flavor of this delightful account would be lost if one relied on Matthew's record alone.

In Matthew 13 (with parallels in Mark 4 and Luke 8), the Lord tells the beautiful parable of the sower that went forth to sow his seed. Some of it, you recall, fell by the wayside and was devoured by birds. Other seeds fell on shallow, rocky ground, and because there was no depth of soil, it sprang up quickly and then, due to the heat of the sun, quickly died. Some of the seed fell among thorns and was presently choked out, while other seed fell upon good ground and produced in varying quantities. In carefully studying this parable, suppose I wish to know what is represented by the "thorns" that can choke out the influence of the seed (the word—Luke 8:11) in my life. Well, in explaining the story, the Lord, according to Matthew's record, teaches that the thorns represent "the care of the world" and "the deceitfulness of riches" (Matthew 13: 22). This involves both the inordinant worry over daily matters, such as food, clothing, etc., and/or the ambition to be wealthy. I can thus learn a valuable lesson about the priorities of life. If I restrict myself to Matthew's account alone. though, I will miss some additional important truths. Mark points out that the thorns also denote "the lusts of other things coming in" (Mark 4:19) and Luke mentions the "pleasures of this life" (Luke 8:14).

The great transfiguration scene is recorded in the 17th chapter of Matthew's gospel. There, on that high mountain, three of the Lord's disciples (Peter, James, and John) observed the Master talking to Moses and Elijah (Matthew 17:3). Would it not be interesting to know the topic of that conversation? Matthew gives us no clue and the student who leaves the record at that point will never know. If one has the industry, however, to examine Luke's parallel (9:31), his curiosity is satisfied. They were discussing Christ's death [decease—Greek, *exodon*] which he was about to accomplish at Jerusalem.

In order to remain in good favor with the Jews, Pilate, the Roman governor, had the custom of occasionally releasing a Jewish prisoner (apparently during a Hebrew feast). Accordingly, at the time of Christ's trial, Pilate set forth two possible release options to the people. Would they prefer to have Jesus set free, or would it be Barabbas? Well, just who was this Barabbas? Matthew simply notes that he was a "notable prisoner" (27:16). But that does not tell the entire story. John's account tells us that Barabbas was a "robber" (18:40) and, significantly, Mark informs us that he was part of a group that had committed murder in the course of attempting to overthrow the government (15:7; cf.: Luke 23:19). What a floodlight of information this throws on the hypocritical charge of the Jews to Pilate: "If you release this man, you are not Caesar's friend...." (John 19:12), as if **they** were! If they were so concerned about Caesar's cause, why ask for the release of a murdering insurrectionist in deference to Him who was so gentle that he even healed the wounded ear of one who came to arrest him (Luke 22:51)?!

Incidentally, this latter event, in concert with other passages, helps to explain a very puzzling circumstance. In his interrogation of Christ, Pilate asked: "Are you the king of the Jews?" He was doubtless trying to determine if Jesus was a political rival. Subsequently, the Lord responded: "My kingdom is not of this world: if my kingdom were of this world, then would my servants fight, that I should not be delivered to the Jews: but now is my kingdom not from hence" (John 18:36). Christ argues that his kingdom is not of a political nature, evidenced by the fact that his disciples would not fight to prevent his arrest by the Jews. Why do you suppose that someone did not immediately step forth and call Christ to account for that statement? An accuser might well have said: "This man claims that his kingdom is not political on the ground that his disciples do not defend him. The fact is, one of his disciples, only a few hours ago, cut off the ear of Malchus, the high priest's servant!" [Cf.: John 18:10]. How is this strange silence to be explained? Easily, if one considers Luke's account. Had such a charge been made, Christ might well have said, "Bring the wounded man forth." How, then, would the Jews have explained the "healed" ear (Luke 22:51)? The last thing they wanted at this time was evidence of a miracle! The charge would have exploded in their faces! The point is, only by doing comparative Bible study is this mystery of "silence" explained.

Once, while doing some study in the book of Kings, I found some very puzzling passages which were illuminated by a consideration of parallel references. Ahab, king of Israel, convinced Jehoshaphat, king of Judah, to accompany him into battle against the Syrians (I Kings 22). As I read this narrative, I wondered why, since the kingdoms of Israel and Judah had been at odds for some seventy-five years, did these two monarchs so easily form a confederation against Syria. I discovered, by means of material elsewhere, that the son of Jehoshaphat had married the daughter of Ahab (Cf.: II Chronicles 21:6). Marriage has made some strange political alliances! And so Ahab and Jehoshaphat decided to engage the Syrians in battle.

Due to the ominous prediction of the prophet Micaiah (that Ahab would not return safely), the king disguised himself, and sent Jehoshaphat, arrayed in royal robes, into the forefront of the conflict. When the enemy soldiers rushed Jehoshaphat's chariot (thinking it was the king of Israel), the monarch cried out! When the captains saw that their intended victim was not Ahab, amazingly, they "turned back from pursuing him" (I Kings 22:33). Why, pray tell? Strange conduct indeed for heathen soldiers. A marvelous parllel in II Chronicles 18 solves the enigma. The record says: "....Jehoshaphat cried out, and **Jehovah helped him; and God moved them to depart from him**" (31). Unless I had taken the time to check my parallel references, I would have missed this thrilling commentary on the providential activity of God in the life of Jehoshaphat!

In Acts 1, the apostle Peter is discussing the fact that it was necessary for someone to be selected to replace the traitor Judas in the office of apostleship. Concerning Judas it is said: "Now this man obtained a field with the reward of his iniquity" (1:18). What is the meaning of this statement? The student will never know unless he does some comparative Bible investigation. The answer is to be found in Matthew 27. There, we are informed that the betrayer "repented himself" [i.e., he had remorse, though not genuine repentance to change his life] and brought back the thirty pieces of silver to the chief priests and elders. He confessed that he had sinned in that he had betrayed innocent blood. But the rulers, of course, cared nothing for this. Judas then, in a fit of depression, threw the money into the sanctuary and went out and hanged himself. The chief priests took that blood-money and with it bought "the potter's field" where strangers were to be buried (3-8). It is, therefore, to this circumstance that Peter alluded in Acts 1:18.

CONCLUSION

The foregoing examples should forcefully illustrate the great importance of doing detailed studies of related Bible accounts. Compare and contrast. Extract every bit of information that you can from the divine record.

In the remaining portion of this chapter, I am going to let you, the student, do some detective work in the scripture text. I'll give you a little help with some of the problems; with others, you'll be on your own. You must use the center-column or marginal references in your Bible, a concordance, dictionary, or other related tools.

Problems To Solve

1. In II Kings 19, Jehovah smote the Assyrian forces of Sennacherib with a mighty defeat. The pagan king returned to Nineveh where he was subsequently slain (while worshipping his god) by two men named Adrammelech and Sharezer). Who were these two men? (Cf.: Isaiah 37:38.)

2. The wicked king Ahab, and his evil wife Jezebel, had Naboth the Jezreelite put to death in order to take his vineyard (I Kings 21:13). What detail does II Kings 9:26 add to this bloody episode?

3. How does John 4:9b shed light on Luke 10:30-37?

4. Shortly before his death, Christ was visiting in the home of Simon the leper of Bethany. While there, a woman anointed his head with expensive ointment (Cf.: Mark 14:3-9). Who was this woman? Who was especially angry about the so-called "waste" of this act? Why was he so indignent?

5. In II Samuel 6, David prepared to bring the "ark of God" to Jerusalem. The ark was placed on a new cart drawn by oxen. On the way, the oxen stumbled and Uzzah put forth his hand to steady the cart. Because of this rash error, he was slain. The incident displeased David (6:8). Is there any evidence that David later evaluated this matter in a more objective light? (Cf.: I Chronicles 15:13.) Explain.

6. According to Matthew's account, when the daughter of Herodius danced, Herod was so pleased that "he promised with an oath to give her whatsoever she should ask" (14:7). Was there any limit to his pledge?

7. A certain man once said to Jesus: "I will follow thee wherever thou goest" (Luke 9:57). What was that man's profession?

8. The mother of Zebedee's sons came to Christ and asked for a favor from the Lord (Matthew 20:20). What were the names of her sons?

9. Shortly before the last supper, Jesus sent two disciples into the city to prepare the place for the passover (Mark 14:13). Who were those two disciples?

10. As Christ prayed in Gethsemane, his disciples slept (Matthew 26:40). What emotion had contributed to that weariness?

11. Judas led a multitude to the garden of Gethsemane where the Lord had gone with his disciples (Matthew 26:47). How did the traitor know **where** to find Jesus?

Chapter 12

TOPICAL BIBLE STUDIES

One of the genuinely challenging, yet fascinating, areas of Bible investigation is that of Topical Studies. By this method, one selects a biblical subject which he wishes to research. He attempts to gather, then to organize, the scriptural data on this particular theme. There are several types of "tools" which he will need in order to effectively pursue a program of topical survey.

"Topical" Bibles and concordances are helpful with this sort of study. Since this type of reference work was not covered in our chapter on "Tools," we will take the liberty of mentioning a few of these here.

Harper's Topical Concordance (Harper & Row)
Family Topical Concordance (Nelson)
Nave's Topical Bible (Baker)
Hitchcock's Topical Bible (Baker)
Zondervan Topical Bible (Zondervan)

Articles on various subjects in Bible dictionaries and encyclopedias can also assist in this area of study, but a word of caution must be offered. If one wishes to become an independent student of the Word, he must not let the research of others **dominate** his personal investigation of a topic. In the final analysis, draw your own conclusions.

There are a couple of ways to approach topical studies.

One may wish, initially, to address some of the very **broad** subjects of scripture. Let us suggest several areas:

I. Special Bible Groups
   A. Great Patriarchs of the Old Testament.
      1. Adam, Abel, Enoch, Noah, Abraham, Isaac, Jacob, Joseph, Moses, etc.
   B. Famous Kings of the Bible.
      1. Kings of the United Kingdom (Saul, David, Solomon).
      2. Kings of Israel.
      3. Kings of Judah.
   C. Prominent Women of the Bible.
      1. Women of the Old Testament—Eve, Sarah, Hannah, Deborah, Ruth, Esther, etc.
      2. Women of the New Testament—Mary, Mary & Martha, Lydia, Phoebe, etc.
   D. Persecuted people of the Bible.
      1. Abel, Joseph, Job, Isaiah, Jeremiah, Daniel, Shadrach, Meshach, Abednego, John the Baptist, Christ, Peter and John, Stephen, Paul, etc.
   E. The Apostles of Christ.
   F. Wicked Rulers.
      1. Nimrod, the Pharaohs, Nebuchadnezzer, Assyrian kings, Herods, etc.

II. Great Doctrinal Themes of the Bible
   A. God, Christ, the Holy Spirit, Man, Angels, Satan, Sin, the Atonement, the Plan of Redemption, the Church, Worship, the Coming of Christ, Judgment.

III. Memorable Prayers of the Bible
   A. David (Psalms 51); Solomon (I Kings 7); Daniel (Daniel 9); Christ (John 17), etc.

IV. Famous Songs in the Bible
   A. Moses (Exodus 15; Deuteronomy 32); Deborah (Judges 5); David (II Samuel 22).

131

V. Great Calls to Service
   A. Abraham (Genesis 12); Moses (Exodus 3); Gideon (Judges 6); Samuel (I Samuel 3); Isaiah (Isaiah 6); Amos (Amos 7); Peter and Andrew (Matthew 4); Paul (Acts 9, 22).

VI. Revivals in the Bible
   A. Joshua (Joshua 5); Samuel (I Samuel 7); Hezekiah (II Kings 18); Josiah (II Kings 22, 23); Nineveh (Jonah 3); Pentecost (Acts 2).

In addition to the broader range of topics, one may wish to concentrate his area of investigation upon a **specific** theme. Here are some topics for possible selection:

I. Names of God
   A. God, Jehovah, Lord, Almighty, etc.

II. Titles of Christ
   A. Lamb of God, Lion from Judah, Shiloh, the Good Shepherd, Son of God, Son of Man, Redeemer, etc.

III. Miracles of Christ
   A. Miracles in nature, miracles over disease, miracles over death, etc.

IV. Parables of Jesus
   A. Kingdom of Parables, Sinner Parables, Forgiveness Parables, Prayer Parables, Stewardship Parables, etc.

V. Great Sermons in the Book of Acts
   A. By Peter (Acts 2, 3, 10, 11, 15); Stephen (Acts 7); Paul (Acts 13, 14, 17, 22, 23, 24, 26).

VI. The Missionary Journeys of Paul
   A. First (Acts 13:4—14:26); Second (Acts 15:40—18:22); Third (Acts 18:23—21:17).

VII. Beatitudes in the New Testament
   A. Beatitudes of Jesus (Matthew 5); Beatitudes in the Book of Revelation (7; cf.: 14:13); etc.

VIII. The "I have sinned" admissions of the Bible
   A. Saul, Judas, Prodigal Son, Achan, David, Pharaoh.

IX. The "I am" statements of the Gospel of John
   A. Bread of Life, True Vine, Door, Shepherd, Way, Truth, Life, Light, etc.

X. Degrees of Faith
   A. Great Faith, Little Faith, Weak Faith, Strong Faith, Perfect Faith, Dead Faith.

Now that we have outlined some possible subjects for topical research, let us get to work. Suppose one wanted to do a topical study on the subject of "God" (a truly ambitious project with which to commence!). He might organize his investigation as follows: [The outline is merely illustrative and is by no means exhaustive.]

I. God—His existence
   A. Man's universal religious tendency.
      1. Acts 17:22-28.
   B. Principle of cause and effect (where there is an effect, there must be an adequate cause).
      1. Hebrews 3:4.
   C. Principle of design (where there is design, there must be a designer).
      1. Psalms 19:1; Romans 1:20.
   D. Conscience (points to a moral law-giver).
      1. Romans 2:14.

II. The Nature of God
   A. He is Spirit, not physical.
      1. John 4:24; Luke 24:39.

B. He is a living Person.
    1. Joshua 3:10; I Thessalonians 1:9).
C. He is invisible.
    1. John 1:18; I Timothy 1:17.
D. He is eternal.
    1. Psalms 90:2; I Timothy 6:18.

III. The Attributes of God
A. He is omnipresent (everywhere present).
    1. Psalms 139:7-12; Acts 17:27, 28.
B. He is (possesses all knowledge).
    1. Proverbs 15:3; Hebrews 4:13.
C. He is omnipotent (all powerful).
    1. Genesis 17:1; Job 42:2; Matthew 19:26.
D. He is absolutely holy.
    1. Habakkuk 1:12; Isaiah 6:3; James 1:13.
E. He is just and righteous.
    1. Genesis 18:25; Psalms 89:14; II Timothy 4:8.
F. He is loving.
    1. John 3:16; I John 4:8.
G. He is benevolent.
    1. Psalms 145:9; Matthew 6:23.
H. He is merciful.
    1. Ephesians 2:4; James 5:11.
I. He is truthful.
    1. John 17:3; I John 5:20; Romans 3:4.

IV. The works of God
A. He is the Creator of the Universe and man.
    1. Genesis 1:1; 1:26; Acts 17:28.
B. He is the Sustainer.
    1. Colossians 1:17; Hebrews 1:3.
C. He has revealed Himself to man.
    1. John 1:18; Hebrews 1:1.
D. He is the Redeemer of Man.
    1. I Timothy 2:3, 4; Titus 1:3.

E. He will judge man according to his works.
   1. Romans 14:10; II Timothy 4:8.

Such studies as the above are tremendously needed in the church today.

Let us say that I am asked to present a series of classes on the topic of "worship." How shall I prepare material for those presentations? I might develop it somewhat as follows:

WORSHIP

I. Some biblical words for "worship"—whether of God, man, or idols.
   A. Hebrew—*segad*—"to bow down."
      1. Daniel 2:46; 3:5, 6; etc.
   B. Hebrew—*atsab*—"to make an idol, worship."
      1. Jeremiah 44:19.
   C. Hebrew—*abad*—"to serve."
      1. II Kings 10:19, 21, etc. [worship of Baal].
   D. Hebrew—*shachah*—"to bow oneself down to."
      1. Genesis 22:5; Exodus 4:31; Isaiah 2:8.
   E. Greek—*proskuneo*—"to kiss towards; reverence."
      1. John 4:24; Matthew 2:2; Acts 7:43.
   F. Greek—*sebomai*—"to revere."
      1. Matthew 15:9; Acts 16:14; 19:27.
   G. Greek—*latreuo*—"to serve, render homage."
      1. Acts 7:42; 24:14.
   H. Greek—*Eusebeo*—"act piously toward."
      1. Acts 17:23.
   I. Greek—*therapeuo*—"to serve."
      1. Acts 17:25.
   J. Greek—*threskeia*—"religious observance."
      1. Colossians 2:18.
   K. Greek—*doxa*—"glory, esteem."
      1. Luke 14:10.

L. Greek—*neokoros*—"temple keeper."
  1. Acts 19:35.

II. Man's instinctive need to worship
   A. The human soul thirsts for God—Psalms 42:1; 63:1.
   B. When man turns from God, he will worship idols or self.

III. True worship must be directed toward the right object; only deity is worthy of worship.
   A. Exodus 20:3; Matthew 4:10; 8:2; I Thessalonians 1:9.

IV. True worship must be characterized by the proper attitude.
   A. Reverence (Hebrews 12:28); humility (James 4:6); thanksgiving (James 1:17); praise (Hebrews 13:15); sincerity (Joshua 24:14).

V. True worship must be in harmony with revealed truth.
   A. John 4:24; 17:17; I Corinthians 4:6; II John 9.
   B. Specific acts of worship are authorized for Christians today—singing (Ephesians 5:19); prayer (I Corinthians 14:15); giving into the church treasury (I Corinthians 16:2); the communion supper (I Corinthians 11:20ff); proclaiming the word (Acts 2:42; 20:7).
   C. Unauthorized worship elicits God's disapproval (Leviticus 10:1ff).

VI. Worship should be a thrilling experience.
   A. Psalms 122:1; 26:8, 12; 116:12-14.

There is much, of course, that might be added to the material given above; it is, however, illustrative of how a subject may be developed.

I once did a study of Christ in terms of the different phases of his existence. It is certainly an interesting approach to the Lord's person and work. I suggest the following for your consideration:

CHRIST

I. As an eternal Being before the creation of the world
   A. The always-existing Word (*logos*).
      1. Genesis 1:1—(suggested in the plural "God").
      2. Genesis 1:26; 3:22; 11:7—(plural pronouns).
      3. Isaiah 9:6—"father of eternity".
      4. Micah 5:2—his goings forth "from everlasting".
      5. John 1:1—Word was (imperfect tense—always was) with God.
      6. John 8:58—before Abraham born, "I am" (always existing).

II. Appearances of Christ in theophanic forms in the Old Testament era
   A. A theophany is a temporary appearance of deity, in contrast to the permanent union involved in the incarnation.
      1. Genesis 16:7, 10—appearance to Hagar.
      2. Genesis 18:1, 13, 17; 22:11ff—appearances to Abraham.
      3. Genesis 19:1; 24—presence at Sodom and Gomorrah.
      4. Genesis 32:24, 28, 30; Hosea 12:4, 5—appearance to Jacob.
      5. Exodus 3:2ff—appearance to Moses.
      6. Judges 6—appearance to Gideon.
      7. I Corinthians 10:4—note Paul's reference to Christ in the wilderness.

III. The incarnate Christ
   A. Jesus, as a being on earth for thirty-three years, was both deity and humanity.

1. His humanity.
   a. Prophesied—Genesis 22:18; Isaiah 7:14.
   b. New Testament affirmation—John 1:14; Romans 1:3; Philippians 2:7, 8; Hebrews 2:11ff.
2. His deity.
   a. Prophesied—Isaiah 7:14; 9:6; Zechariah 13:7.
   b. New Testament affirmation—John 1:1; 10:30; 20:28; Titus 2:13; Hebrews 1:8.

IV. The reigning Christ
   A. Prophesied—II Samuel 7:12-16; Isaiah 9:6, 7; Zechariah 6:13.
   B. New Testament affirmation—Matthew 2:2; 21:5; 27:11.
   C. Christ's kingdom not political in nature—John 18:36.
   D. Kingdom entered by "new birth"—John 3:3-5; Colossians 1:13.

V. The final state
   A. Christ returns the reign to the Father.
      1. Between Pentecost and the Judgment, Christ exercises "all authority"—Matthew 28:18; Ephesians 1:20ff.
      2. Only the Father is excepted from that rule—I Corinthians 15:27.
      3. After all things have been subjected to the Son (the consummation of His present reign), then will the Son Himself be subjected to the Father—I Corinthians 15:28.
      4. The implication of this passage suggests that by the incarnation, Christ, in some way, became identified **with us** forevermore—Cf.: Romans 8:17. What an astounding commentary on the love of Christ!

I suggest that such a five point, topical study of the work of Christ would open the minds of many to magnificent truths that they've not considered previously.

One of the more fascinating topical studies that I've done is an investigation of the several names used for God in the Old Testament. There are some very wonderful points involved in such a survey. Note the following:

NAMES OF GOD IN THE OLD TESTAMENT

I. God (Hebrew *El*, *Elah*, or *Elohim*)
    A. The term denotes "strength" or "power".
    B. It especially emphasizes the power of God in such acts as the creation—Genesis 1:1.
    C. In the plural form *Elohim*, the trinity is latent—Cf.: Genesis 1:26; John 1:1.

II. Lord (Hebrew *Adon* or *Adonai*)
    A. The word suggests "master" or "ruler".
    B. Its emphasis is the authority of the Lord; the plural form *adonai* is only used of God in the Old Testament.
    C. The word stresses the obedience that man owes to his Master—Malachi 1:6; cf.: Hebrews 5:8, 9.

III. Almighty God (*El Shaddai*)
    A. *El* means "strong" and *shaddai* may derive from the noun *shad*, "breast," hence "to nourish." The name may thus suggest "him who is strong to nourish, to satisfy his people" Cf.: Genesis 49:24, 25; Isaiah 60:15, 16; 66:10-13.
    B. God Almighty is able to abundantly supply all the needs of His people—Philippians 4:19.

IV. Most High, or Most High God (*El Elyon*)
    A. The distinctive meaning suggested in this title is revealed in Genesis 14:17-24—"the most high God,

possessor of heaven and earth".

    B. This was the common name of God among Gentile nations—Cf.: Deuteronomy 32:8; Daniel 4:17; Isaiah 14:13.

V. Everlasting God (*El Olam*)

    A. He is eternal in nature—Psalms 90:2.

    B. God is the deity of everlasting things—Genesis 21: 33; Cf.: Ephesians 1:9, 10; 3:3-6.

VI. Jehovah (*Yahweh*)

    A. Jehovah is derived from the Hebrew *havah* meaning "to be" or "being." It denotes God's self-existent nature. Most frequently used name of God in the Old Testament—6,823 times. Cf.: Genesis 2:4; Exodus 3:14, 15; 6:2, 3.

    B. Jehovah is the "covenant" name; the redemptive designation of Israel's God. Jehovah is the loving, revealed, saving God of those who respond to His holy will.

VII. Jehovah God (*Yahweh Elohim*)

    A. Denotes God's relationship to man as: Creator—Genesis 2:7-15; Master—Genesis 2:16, 17; Ruler—Genesis 2:18-24; Redeemer—Genesis 3:8-15.

    B. Jehovah's relationship to Israel—Genesis 24:7; Exodus 3:15, 18; Deuteronomy 12:1.

VIII. Lord of Hosts (*Yahweh Sabaoth*)

    A. Used with special reference to warfare or service.

    B. Indicates a display of God's power and glory—Psalms 24:10; 46:7, 11.

    C. "Hosts" may suggest angels, or all heavenly powers available for the needs of the Lord's people.

In addition to the names surveyed above, it is interesting to note that there are eight uses of the name "Jehovah" as a compound with other expressions. These forms contain some enriching thoughts.

1. *Jehovah-jireh* (Genesis 22:13, 14) means "Jehovah will provide." As the Lord provided Abraham with a ram to offer in the place of Isaac, so He provided His Son to die in our stead. Additionally, He has provided us with all things necessary for life and godliness (Cf.: Romans 8:32; II Peter 1:3).

2. *Jehovah-rophe* (Exodus 15:26) denotes "Jehovah heals." When Israel marched into the wilderness and came to Marah, they found bitter waters that they could not drink (Exodus 15:23). By a miracle, God "healed" the waters from bitter to sweet. Similarly, the Lord, by the gift of His Son, has provided **spiritual** healing for the nations through His redemptive plan.

3. *Jehovah-nissi* (Exodus 17:8-15) suggests "Jehovah is our banner." In their wilderness trek, Israel was assaulted by the hostile Amalekites, descendants of Esau. In spite of the fact that the Hebrews were an inexperienced and ill-equipped military force, the Lord gave them a great victory over their enemies. He was their banner of triumph! Through Christ, we become more than conquerors over all opposition (Romans 8:37; Revelation 12:11).

4. *Jehovah-m'kaddesh* (Leviticus 20:8) means "Jehovah who sanctifies." The book of Leviticus has to do with the consecration of God's redeemed nation. The term "sanctify," in its various original forms, appears some 700 times in the Old Testament. Those who would be in intimate communion with the holy God must be sanctified—set apart as holy ones. Certain Old Testament ordinances were designed to accomplish that, looking forward, of course, to the coming of Christ and the sanctification effected once for all by the offering of His blood (Hebrews 10:10; cf.: Ephesians 5:26).

5. *Jehovah-shalom* (Judges 6:24) affirms that "Jehovah is our peace." When the children of Israel did evil in the Lord's sight, He sold them into the hand of their enemies and they were sorely oppressed (Cf.: Judges 6:1ff). During these dark hours, the Messenger of the Lord appeared to Gideon and

gave him a promise of deliverance. In anticipation of that hope, Gideon built an altar and called it "Jehovah-*shalom*." Today, in a much higher sense, God is our peace. Through Christ, who effected peace by the blood of His cross (Colossians 1:20), we can be in harmony with our Creator (Cf.: Romans 5:1).

6. *Jehovah-rohi* (Psalms 23:1) is the beautiful expression, "Jehovah is my Shepherd." God is the kind Shepherd who sustains and protects His people (review the material on this psalm in chapter 7). Even so, Christ is our good Shepherd who will lead us safely home (Cf.: John 10).

7. *Jehovah-tsidkenu* (Jeremiah 23:6) means "Jehovah our righteousness." We, as fallen creatures, cannot stand before God and demand a merited justification. It was thus necessary that Jehovah send His Son, who would be able to do for us what we are unable to accomplish on our own. In view of this, Jeremiah prophesied of the "righteous Branch" who would be raised up out of the lineage of David. He would "reign as king and deal wisely, and shall execute justice and righteousness in the land" (23:5). This, of course, was Jesus Christ. When we, in loving obedience, respond to Heaven's will, on the basis of what Jesus did at Calvary, God accounts us as righteous; He pardons our sins (Cf.: Romans 3:21ff).

8. *Jehovah-shammah* (Ezekiel 48:35) means "Jehovah is there." Fourteen years after the conquest of Jerusalem (586 B.C.), the prophet Ezekiel, a captive in Babylon, saw a vision of the restoration and glory of the kingdom of God. It was set forth under the imagery of the rebuilding of the temple (Cf.: Ezekiel 40—48). The name of the city of that wonderful temple is called by the prophet, "Jehovah is there," in the final words of his narrative. The vision finds its fulfillment, of course, in the establishment of the church of the New Testament age, also figuratively called the temple of God (I Corinthians 3:16; II Corinthians 6:16). This (the church) is the place, therefore, where Jehovah is to be found today. The person who wants fellowship with his Creator will thus seek such within the house of God, the church of Christ (I Timothy 3:15).

Though our study of these titles of God has been quite limited, one can certainly see the possibilities in this type of biblical exploration.

As a further expansion of his knowledge of this method of Bible study, the student is urged to carefully pursue the following exercises.

ASSIGNMENT

A Brief Survey of Sin

Sin Defined:

Sin is:

_____	I John 3:4
_____	I John 5:17
_____	Jeremiah 11:10
_____	James 4:17
_____	Romans 14:23
_____	I Samuel 15:23
_____	Leviticus 10:1,2
_____	Hebrews 9:7 (ASV,fn)

How sin affects man:

Sin:

_____	Isaiah 59:1,2
_____	Proverbs 14:34
_____	Hebrews 3:13
_____	James 1:15
_____	Revelation 21:27
_____	John 8:34
_____	Isaiah 30:1

143

The proper attitude toward sin:

Sin should be:

_____ Proverbs 28:13
_____ I Corinthians 6:18
_____ Psalms 38:18
_____ Romans 12:9
_____ Colossians 3:5
_____ II Timothy 2:19

The sins of the non-Christian will be forgiven when the sinner:

_____ Mark 16:16
_____ Acts 2:38
_____ Romans 6:17
_____ Ephesians 5:26
_____ I Peter 3:21

The sins of the child of God will be forgiven when he/she:

_____ Acts 8:22
_____ James 5:16
_____ I John 1:9

Chapter 13

BIOGRAPHICAL BIBLE STUDIES

Jesus once asked, "Who do men say that the Son of man is?" The disciples responded that some thought He was John the Baptizer, or Elijah, or perhaps Jeremiah (Matthew 16:14). Were certain traits of those great prophets observed in Christ? In order to appreciate this passage, must one know something about John, Elijah, and Jeremiah? Christ declared, "As were the days of Noah, so shall be the coming of the Son of man" (Matthew 24:37). What was significant about Noah and his times? Is there profit in knowing about that situation?

It is estimated that there are some 2,930 different men and women mentioned in the Bible. Some of them are mentioned but once, and there is no additional information about them whatever. Of others, however, much was written. From the passages cited above, it is obvious that biographical data are of vital importance to the understanding of certain biblical contexts. Paul's argument concerning Abraham's faith being reckoned unto him for righteousness, prior to his circumcision, and his subsequent admonition that we "walk in the steps of faith" of that patriarch (Romans 4:1ff), presume that the reader is familiar with the details of Abraham's life.

There is much to be learned from the lives of men and women (both good and evil) who are mentioned in the Bible. The great faith of biblical heroes encourages us to "run with patience the race that is set before us" (Hebrews 12:1). The mistakes of those who ignored Jehovah's instructions and suffered the consequences thereof, are sober reminders of the seriousness of living uprightly before our sovereign Creator (Cf.: I Corinthians 10:5ff; Luke 17:32).

The study of Bible biographies is a fascinating endeavor, but like other areas of research, it must be done in a careful, systematic fashion. As a preliminary approach to this area of study, we would recommend the following guidelines in gathering the sacred information on prominent persons within the Scripture record.

First, assemble all of the biblical passages which mention the particular subject of your inquiry. A word of caution—be sure that your references all relate to the same person. Many diverse Bible characters have the same name; there are thirty Old Testament men named Zechariah; five men named James, and five named John, in the New Testament, etc. Suppose, for example, one wishes to study the life of Jehoshaphat, the king of Judah. He should collect the following references as sources for his research—I Kings 15:24; 22:1ff; II Kings 1:17; 3:1, 7-27; 8:16, 24, 25; 12:18; II Chronicles 17-20. Usually, the better Bible dictionaries will list all of the passages pertaining to the people listed in those reference works.

Second, one should look carefully at the name or names of the Bible character he is studying; for names, in the divine record, are frequently of great significance. Abram, meaning "exalted father," was changed to Abraham, "father of a multitude" (Genesis 17:5); Jacob ("one that takes by the heel") had his name changed to Israel ("he who strives with God") (Genesis 32:28). Solomon ("peace") was also known as Jedidiah ("beloved of Jehovah") (II Samuel 12:24, 25); Saul became known as Paul (Acts 13:9, 13), etc.

Third, carefully note the ancestry of your subject. It is helpful to know that the parents of Athaliah, Judah's wicked queen, were the infamous Ahab and Jezebel of Israel. Paul's ancestry is of considerable importance to his argument relating to certain Judaizers troubling the Philippian brethren (Cf.: Philippians 3:4ff). Timothy's background is essential to understanding why Paul imposed the Jewish rite of circumcision upon that lad (Cf.: Acts 16:1-3).

Fourth, observe the environment and training which your Bible character had in youth. Abraham's great fidelity to Jehovah truly shines forth when one learns that he came out of a pagan background (Cf.: Joshua 24:2). Similarly, note the idolatrous influences in Rachel's family as evidenced by the fact that she stole her father's teraphim when she and Jacob fled from Paddan—aram (Genesis 31:19). The sacrifices of Moses are much appreciated when one learns that Israel's great deliverer was raised as a prince of Egypt, "instructed in all the wisdom of the Egyptians" (Acts 7:22), and that he valued his mission greater than the treasures of that heathen land (Cf.: Hebrews 11:26). The dedication of the Lord's disciples, James and John, is also illuminated when one discovers that prior to following Christ, these men were involved in a successful fishing business. They even had "hired servants" in that enterprise (Mark 1:20). Moreover, Simon Peter was a "partner" in the company (Luke 5:10)!

Fifth, attempt to determine the character traits of your subject. For example, how would you evaluate the temperament of Moses relative to the incident wherein he killed the Egyptian and hid his body in the sand (Exodus 2:12)? Do not certain passages in the book of Jeremiah suggest that this prophet was given to periods of melancholy (9:1ff; 20:14-18)? It is interesting to note how Elijah appears to vacillate between periods of courageousness, such as when he confronts the prophets of Baal (I Kings 18:16ff), and times of fearfulness, as when he fled from Jezebel (I Kings 19:1ff). A survey of the passages which reveal the transformation of Peter from an impetuous, rather unstable individual (if we may say so respectfully)—ready to defend Christ with his sword one moment, only to deny him hours later—to the "rock-like" character he eventually became, is truly remarkable.

Sixth, observe the friends and close associates of your character. For instance, no study of the life of David would be complete without a consideration of this great friendship with Jonathan, the son of king Saul (I Samuel 18:1-4; 20; 23: 16-18; II Samuel 9:1). In considering the life of Paul, it would be crucial to observe his relationships with Barnabas, Silas, Timothy, etc. Whomever a person selects for his or her friends is often a revealing character index.

Seventh, in surveying Bible personalities, notice the great events, crises, etc., that occurred during their lives. Moses' life is characterized by several such circumstances—his flight from Egypt (Exodus 2); the meeting with Jehovah at the burning bush (Exodus 3); his confrontation with Pharaoh when he demanded the release of Israel (Exodus 5); the crisis of Israel's murmuring in the wilderness (Exodus 16); his sin in smiting the rock at Meribah (Numbers 20), etc. The dramatic events in Elijah's ministry are more exciting than any novel ever written. The critical situations of a man's life either forge him into the type of person who can accomplish great things for Jehovah, or they will be his undoing. Such events are, therefore, vital components of biographical studies.

Eighth, note the influence that your study-subject had upon his/her contemporaries. For instance, what impact did Jonah, the unwilling missionary, have upon the city of ancient Nineveh? That community, due to his influence, survived one hundred and fifty years longer than the prophet's initial forty-day condemnation warning! (Cf.: Jonah; Nahum). If one were making a character study of Judah's king, Josiah, a major portion of it would deal with the great reforms that the monarch was able to bring about among the Lord's people (Cf.: II Kings 22, 23; II Chronicles 34, 35). The evil influence of Jeroboam, the son of Nebat, is carefully documented in the record of Kings when the divine narrative, more than twenty times, calls attention to this wicked ruler who "made Israel to sin."

No study of the life of Christ would be complete without a consideration of the Master's influence; first, upon His own generation; then, upon the world since that time. If one were to reflect upon the Lord's impact on others, as revealed in the

New Testament, he might organize the material as follows: The influence of Jesus: (1) Upon the Disciples; (2) Upon the Multitudes; (3) Upon His Enemies; (4) Upon those Ensnared in Sin.

Ninth, one should carefully note the spiritual growth (or lack of it) in the subject of his inquiry. Mention was made earlier of Peter. At first he was a vacillating disciple, denying his Master. Later, though, he could stand in the face of hostile opposition and exclaim, "We must obey God rather than men." The growth of Nicodemus, as revealed in the book of John, is quite encouraging. First, he seeks out the Lord by night (John 3:1ff); next, he speaks up in Jesus' defense, suggesting that it is improper to condemn a man without first hearing his case (John 7:50, 51); finally, he boldly joins with Joseph of Arimathaea in preparing the Savior's body for burial (John 19:39). There is a real maturing process here!

Tenth, in looking at a biblical character, one should notice if his subject had any particular besetting sins which played a significant role in his life. Did not, for instance, both Samson and David have a weakness for women that cast a dark shadow over their careers? And what of Peter and James? They both struggled with that bigotry which was so common to the Jewish mind (Cf.: Galatians 2:11ff). How wonderfully might Moses and Aaron have thrilled to entering into the Promised Land had they not weakened in faith and failed to sanctify the Lord in Israel's sight (Cf.: Numbers 20:12). Surely Judas must have had some worthy traits, as evidenced by the fact that Christ selected him as an apostle. Why did he make such a drastic change in his disposition toward the Lord? Was he motivated solely by covetousness? In his interesting volume, *The Training of the Twelve*, A.B. Bruce argues that the flaws in Judas went considerably beyond greed. Perhaps disappointment, jealousy, etc. ate deeply into his soul.

Eleventh, one might finally ask: What significant lessons can I learn from this Bible character? We suggest that the following people, some good and some not so good, teach these valuable lessons. From the lives of Abel and Cain one learns the wisdom of worshipping God exactly as He has prescribed (Hebrews 11:4). Abraham teaches us how to walk in the "steps of faith" (Romans 4:12). Joseph and Esther instruct us that God can use us to accomplish great things even under adverse circumstances and when we are unaware of His providential guidance (Genesis 45:5, 7, 8; Esther 4:14). From David we learn that even though sin has marred our lives, we can still overcome and be useful to the cause of Jehovah (Cf.: I Kings 15:5). Solomon is an example of the folly of marrying out of the faith (I Kings 11:1-4), and Absalom's life reveals that the road of blind ambition leads to a disastrous conclusion (II Samuel 18). Paul shows us how to learn contentment in all of life's situations (Philippians 4:11); and of course the Lord Jesus, among many wonderful things, demonstrated that service to others is the commentary on love (Philippians 2:5ff).

In so many ways, the study of Bible personalities can be a tremendous boon to our lives.

PUTTING THE METHOD TO WORK

As an example of the procedure we have presented above, let us attempt to assemble some of the biographical data relative to the apostle Paul. Due to space limitations, we will need to be brief, but you can get the idea.

A BIOGRAPHICAL STUDY OF PAUL THE APOSTLE

I. Birth and Early Life
   A. Names
      1. Hebrew *Saulos*, "asked for" (Cf.: I Samuel 1:11).
      2. Roman name *Paulos*, "little."
   B. Parentage and Family

1. From tribe of Benjamin; both parents Hebrews (Philippians 3:5).
2. Inherited status of Roman citizen (Acts 22:28).
3. Had a sister (Acts 23:16).
4. No evidence that Paul was ever married.

C. Place of Birth
1. Born in Tarsus of Cilicia (Acts 21:39; 22:3).

D. Early Training
1. Brought up as a Pharisee (Acts 23:6; 26:5; Philippians 3:5).
2. Evidence of Greek education (Acts 17:28; I Corinthians 15:33; Titus 1:12).
3. Learned trade of tent-maker (Acts 18:3).
4. Trained in law of Moses (Cf.: Deuteronomy 6:4-9).
5. At early age, went to Jerusalem to study under Gamaliel (Acts 22:3).
6. Zealous for God (Acts 22:3).
7. Blameless in the law's righteousness (Philippians 3:6).
8. Advanced in Jews' religion (Galatians 1:14).
9. Well-known by all the Jews (Acts 26:4, 5).

II. Attitude Toward the Christian Religion
A. A Persecutor
1. Consented to death of Stephen (Acts 7:58).
2. Laid waste the church (Acts 8:1, 3).
3. Was sincere in persecuting the Way (Acts 22:4; 23:1; 26:9).
4. Disrupted Christian worship; pressured saints to deny the Lord (Acts 26:10, 11).
5. Persecuted Christians unto foreign cities (Acts 26:11), beating, imprisoning, and killing them (Acts 22:19).
6. Hostile to both men and women (Acts 8:3; 9:2; 22:4).

7. Persecuted church beyond measure (Galatians 1:13).
8. The memories stayed with him for years (I Corinthians 15:9; Ephesians 3:8; I Timothy 1:15).

B. His Conversion
1. In route from Jerusalem to Damascus to persecute Christians (Acts 9:1ff).
2. Saw Christ on the way (Acts 9:17; I Corinthians 15:8).
3. Led to city where he fasted and prayed three days.
4. Heard gospel from Ananias; was baptized to wash away his sins (Acts 22:16).
5. After certain days, commenced to proclaim Jesus as the Christ (Acts 9:20).

III. Paul as a Preacher of the Gospel
A. The Early Years
1. Preached in the synagogues of Damascus (Acts 9:20).
2. Journeyed to Arabia, back to Damascus (Galatians 1:17).
3. Fled from Damascus to Jerusalem (Acts 9:23), stayed in Jerusalem fifteen days (Galatians 1:18).
4. While praying in temple, instructed to go forth to Gentiles (Acts 22:17-21).
5. Went to his native Tarsus (Acts 9:30)—remained there eight to ten years.
6. Came to Antioch of Syria; labored with Barnabus for a year (Acts 11:25, 26).

B. The Missionary Journeys
1. First Journey (Acts 13:4—14:26)
   a. Cyprus, Asia Minor—possibly two years.
   b. Goes to Jerusalem regarding matter of keep-

ing law of Moses (Acts 15:1ff).
   2. Second Journey (Acts 15:40—18:22)
      a. Along with Silas, westward across Asia Minor.
      b. Joined by Timothy (Acts 16:1-3) and Luke ("we" 16:10, 11).
      c. On into Europe.
      d. Total time—approximately four years.
   3. Third Journey (Acts 18:23—21:17)
      a. Westward through Asia.
      b. Over to Macedonia—joined by Titus (II Corinthians 7:5, 6), possibly Timothy (I Timothy 1:1).
      c. To Philippi, joined by Luke (Acts 20:6); from there to Asia.
      d. Concludes at Jerusalem—some three to four years.
C. The Final Years
   1. Accused by Jewish enemies, arrested in Jerusalem (Acts 21:33).
   2. Taken to Caesarea, imprisoned two years (Acts 24:27).
   3. Appeal to Caesar (Acts 25:9-12).
   4. Journey to Rome (Acts 27:1—28:16).
   5. Two years awaiting trial.
   6. Released; indications that he went to Spain (Cf.: Romans 15:24, *Letter to Clement*, 95 A.D.).
   7. Beheaded in Rome—c. 67 A.D.

IV. Paul's Writings
A. Galatians
   1. Written from Antioch, c. 49 A.D. (Acts 14:26).
   2. Argues release from law of Moses.
B. I Thessalonians
   1. Written from Corinth (Acts 18:5-11), c. 52, 53.

153

    2. Encouragement in view of Lord's Return.

C. II Thessalonians
    1. Written from Corinth (Acts 18:5-11), 52, 53.
    2. Corrects misunderstanding regarding I Thessalonians relative to Lord's Coming.

D. I Corinthians
    1. From Ephesus (Acts 19:8-22), spring 54, 55.
    2. Problems of the local church.

E. II Corinthians
    1. From Macedonia (Acts 20:1), fall 54, 55.
    2. Defense of Paul's apostleship; encouragement to complete collection for needy saints.

F. Romans
    1. From Corinth, Greece (Acts 20:2, 3), 56 A.D.
    2. Justification through gospel (Romans 1:16).

G. Philemon
    1. From Rome during first imprisonment (Acts 28); 62.
    2. Instructions concerning a runaway slave.

H. Colossians
    1. From Rome (Acts 28), 62 A.D.
    2. Defense of supremacy of Christ against heresy.

I. Ephesians
    1. From Rome (Acts 28), 62 A.D.
    2. God's eternal purpose as fulfilled in Christ.

J. Philippians
    1. From Rome (Acts 28), 62, 63 A.D.
    2. Intimate letter to Paul's "beloved" brethren.

K. I Timothy
    1. From Macedonia (1:3) after Paul's release from his Roman confinement (Acts 28), c. 64 A.D.
    2. Practical instruction to the young evangelist.

L. Titus
    1. Possibly from Macedonia while proceeding toward Nicopolis (3:1), c. 64 A.D.
    2. Church organization, practical counsel.

M. II Timothy
   1. From Paul's final Roman imprisonment where he is awaiting execution (4:6-8), c. 66, 67 A.D.
   2. Concluding exhortation to fidelity.
N. Note: some believe that Paul authored Hebrews. Since, however, the Holy Spirit left that document anonymous, it is wiser to concur.

V. Some Valuable Lessons from the Life of Paul
   A. The providence of God was at work in the early training of Paul (Cf.: Galatians 1:15).
   B. To persecute a Christian is to persecute Christ (Acts 9:4).
   C. One may be sincere, yet wrong (Acts 23:1; 26:9).
   D. The pardon of Christ can cover all sins genuinely repented of, including murder, blasphemy (Acts 26:10; I Timothy 1:13).
   E. Heredity background does not insure salvation (Philippians 3:4-6).
   F. One must be willing to sacrifice all for Christ (Philippians 3:7ff).
   G. Christ must be the center of one's life (Philippians 1:21).
   H. With the Lord's help, the Christian can even bravely face death (Philippians 1:21; II Timothy 4:6, 7).

Questions

1. Cite two New Testament examples which presuppose some knowledge of biographical data relating to Old Testament personalities.

2. Name at least two values in studying biographies of Bible personalities.

3. What is the first step in doing a biographical study?

4. By doing some research (in commentaries, etc.), see if you can determine the spiritual significance in the change of Jacob's name to "Israel."

5. What do you know of Rachel's religious background?

6. What was Josiah's administration noted for?

7. How is the spiritual growth of Nicodemus revealed in the book of John. Cite passages.

8. Name one great lesson that can be learned from the life of David.

9. In what "trade" was Paul trained as a youngster. Cite passage.

10. Give the New Testament references that mark the beginning and ending of Paul's three missionary journeys. Note these at the appropriate places in the margins of your Bible.

11. List three valuable lessons learned from the life of the apostle Paul.